ISBN-13: 978-1515114444

ISBN-10: 1515114449

DEDICATION

To my Mother, who has always held imagination to its highest regard and who has never imposed her own conclusions. Free thought is her only encouragement and love her only intention.
With immense gratefulness I dedicate this book.

Anthropomorphism

is the attribution of human form or other characteristics to beings other than humans, particularly deities and animals. Personification is the related attribution of human form and characteristics to abstract concepts such as nations and natural forces likes seasons and the weather. Both have ancient roots as storytelling and artistic devices. Most cultures have traditional fables with anthropomorphized animals as characters.

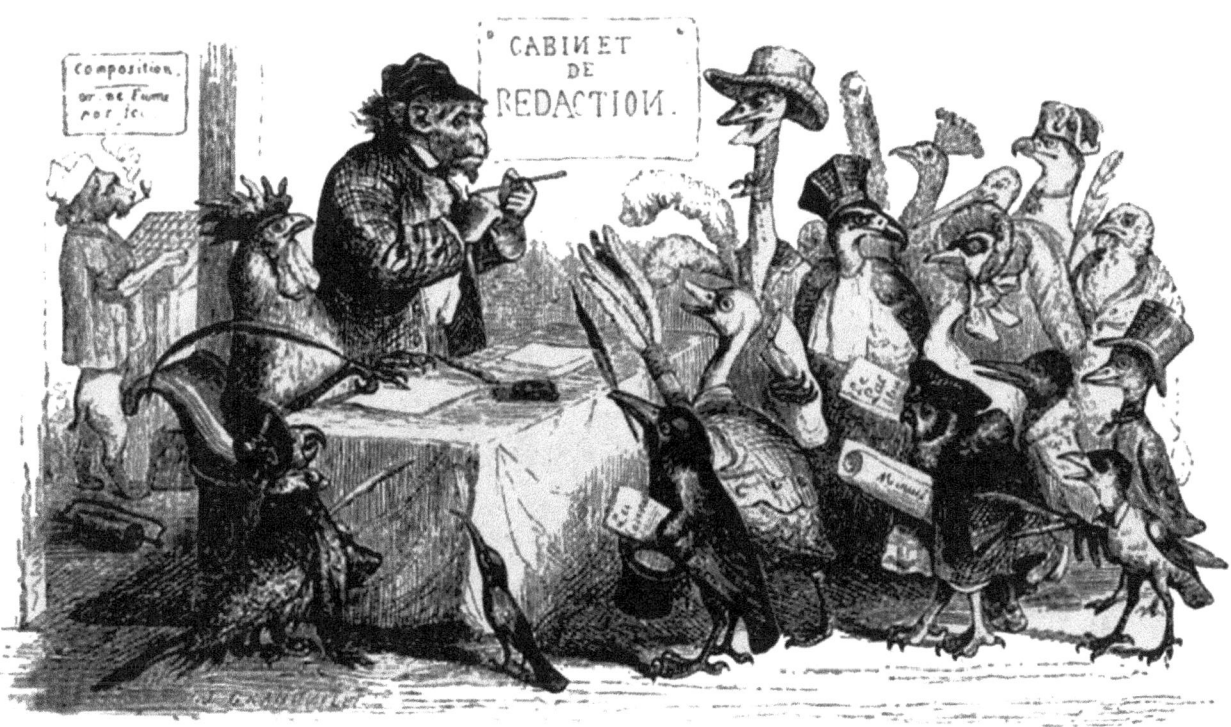

Zoomorphism

is the shaping of something in animal form or terms.
Examples include:
Art that imagines humans as non-human animals.
Art that portrays one species of animal like another species of animal.
Art that creates patterns using animal imagery, or animal style
Deities depicted in animal form, such as exist in ancient Egyptian religion.

Therianthropy

the ability to shapeshift into animal form. Attributing animal form or other animal characteristics to anything other than an animal; similar to but broader than anthropomorphism

The tendency of viewing human behavior in terms of the behavior of animals, contrary to anthropomorphism, which views animal or non-animal behavior in human terms.

The mythological ability of human beings to metamorphose into animals by means of shapeshifting. It is possible that cave drawings found at Les Trois Frères, in France, depict ancient beliefs in the concept. The most well-known form of therianthropy is found in stories concerning werewolves.

ACKNOWLEDGMENTS

I would like to acknowledge the imagination and incredible talent of the 19th century French caricaturist Jean Ignace Isidore Gérard Grandville or J.J. Grandville, who I have featured in this presentation.

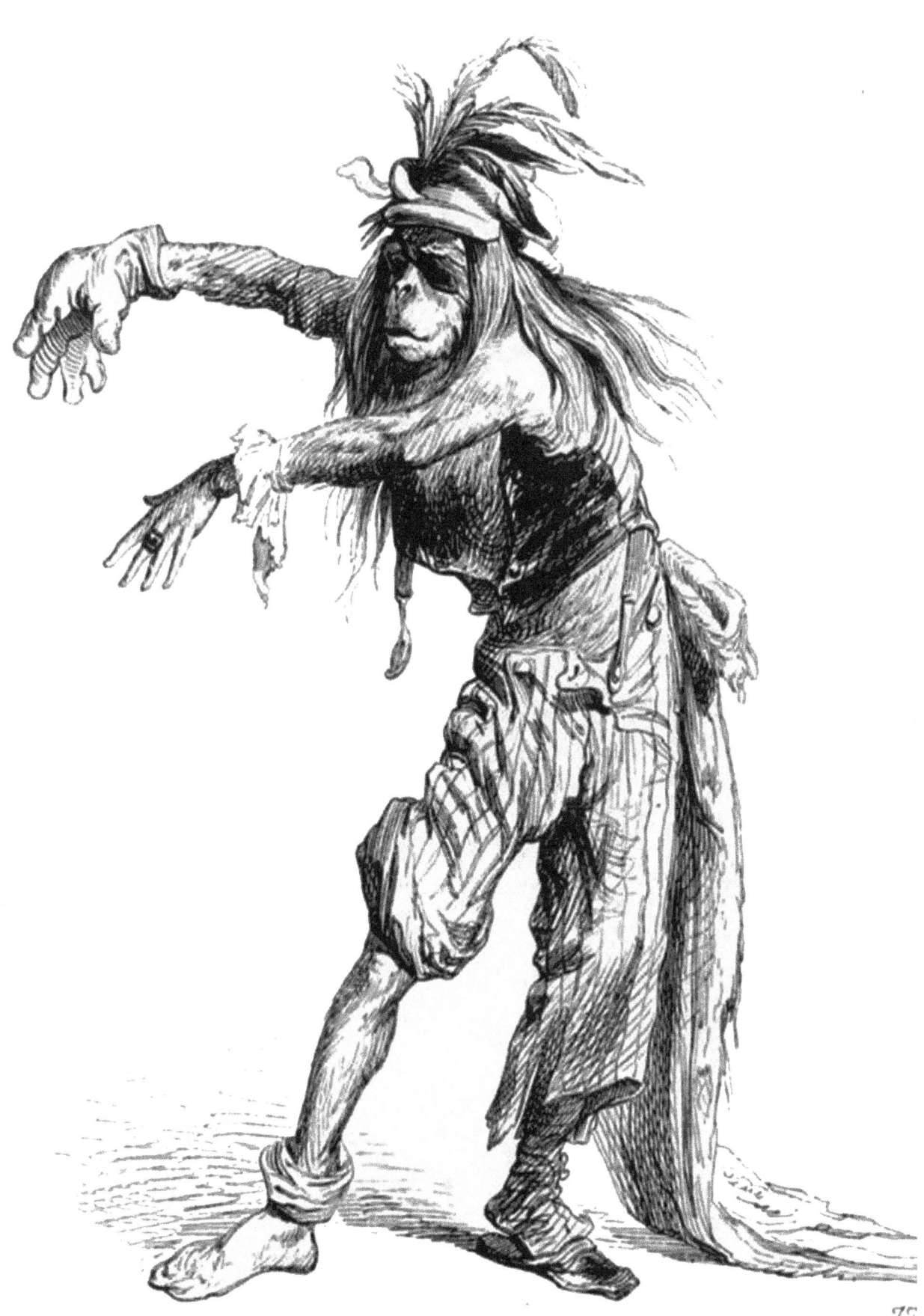

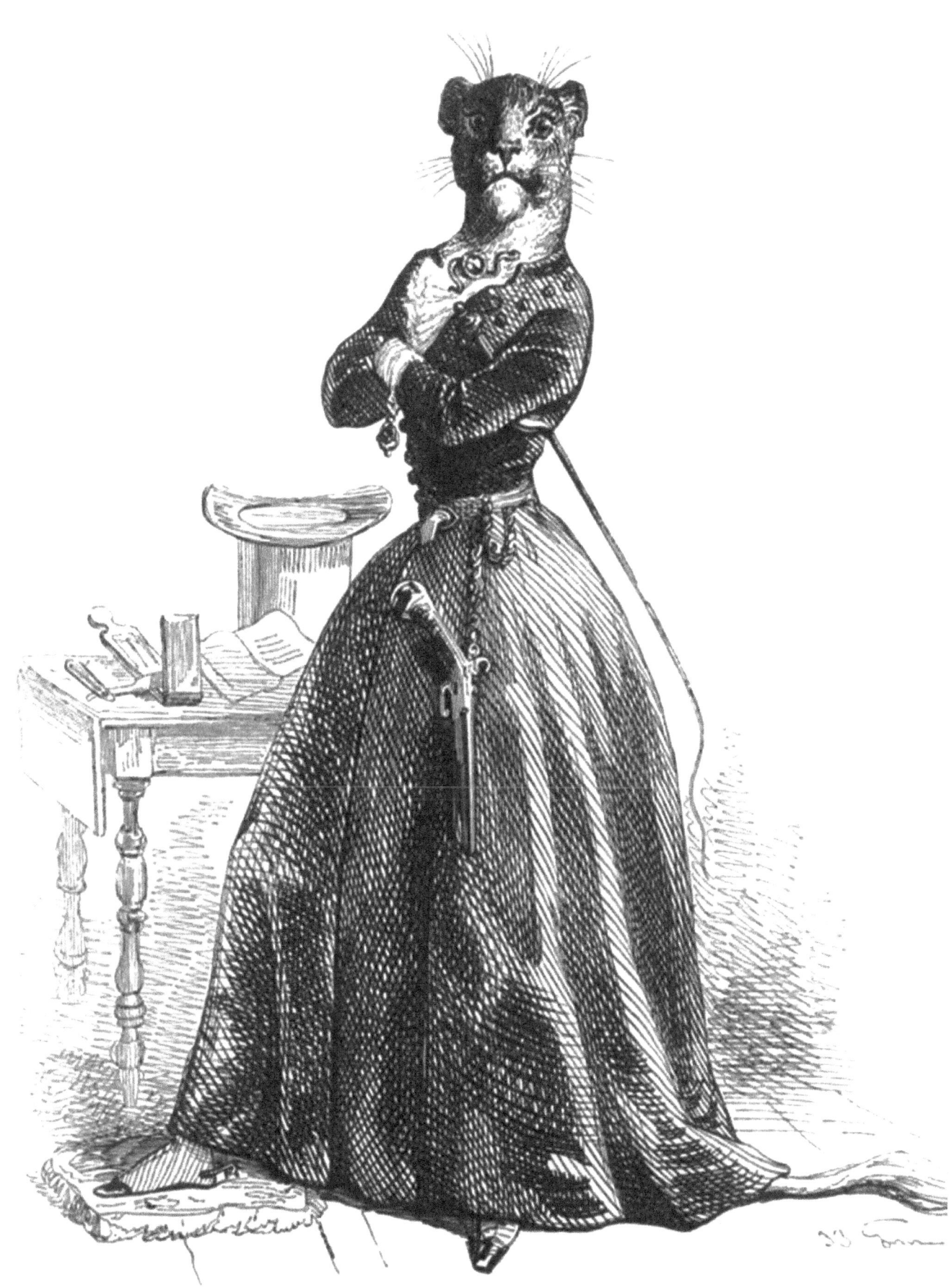

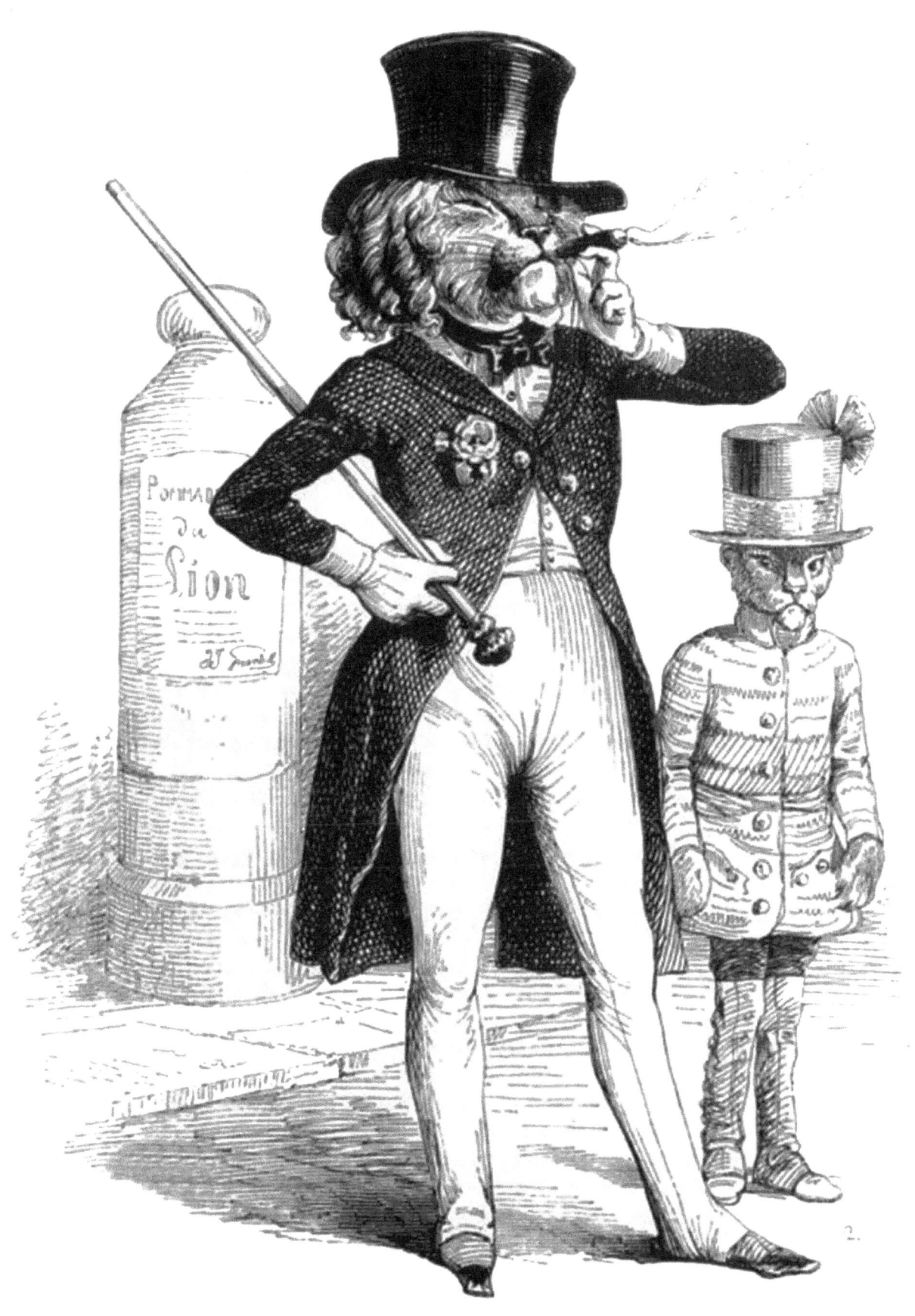

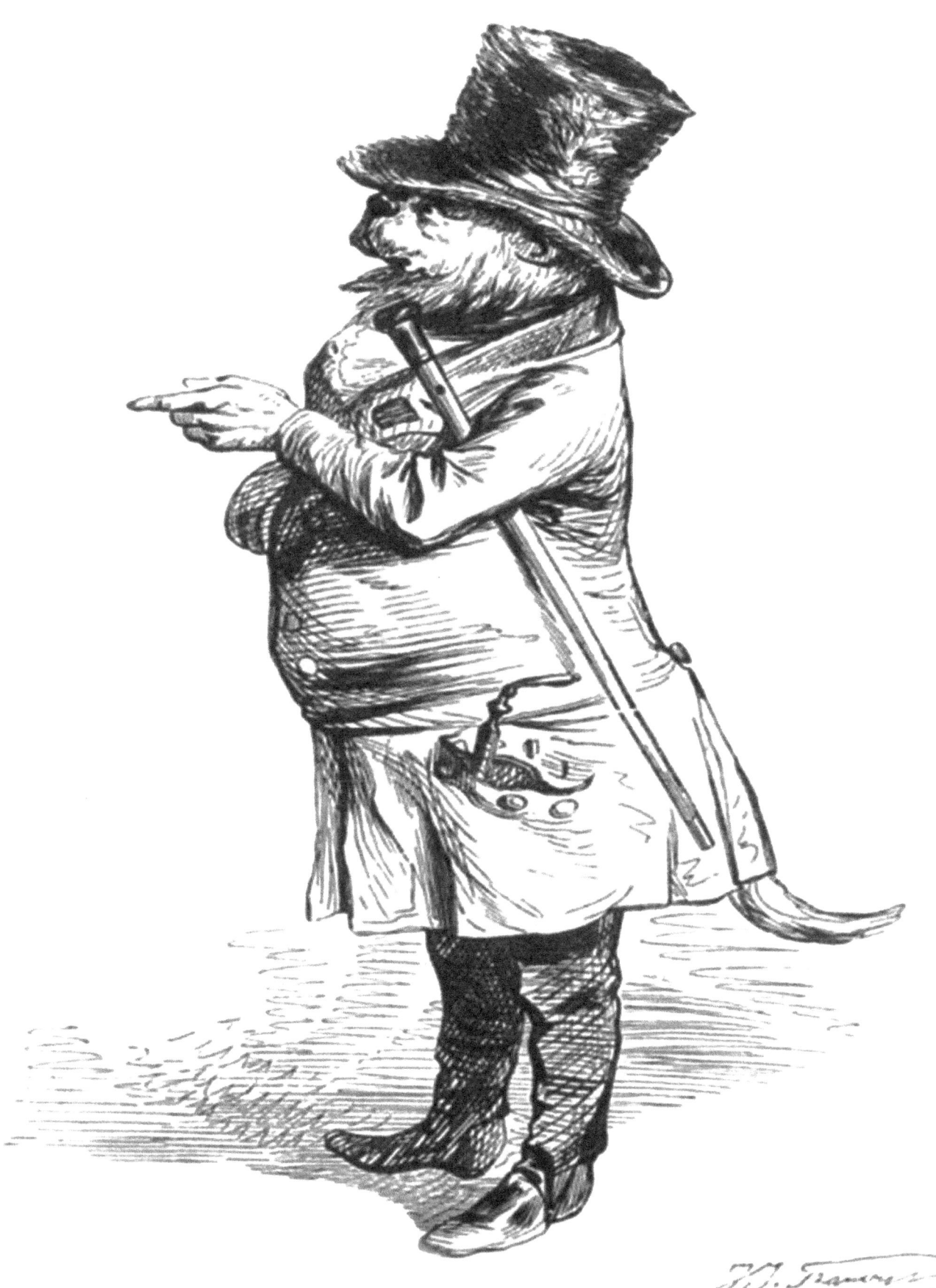

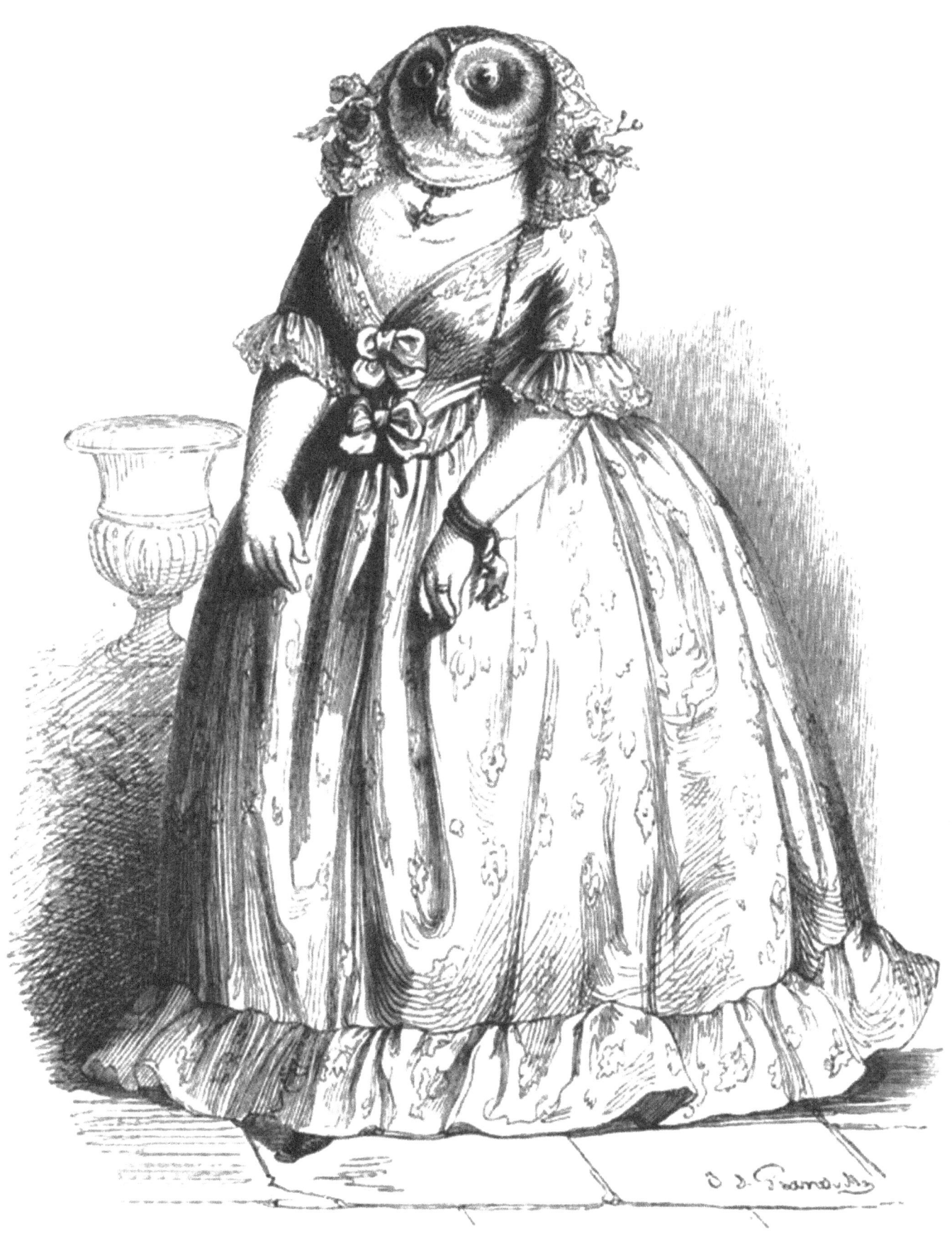

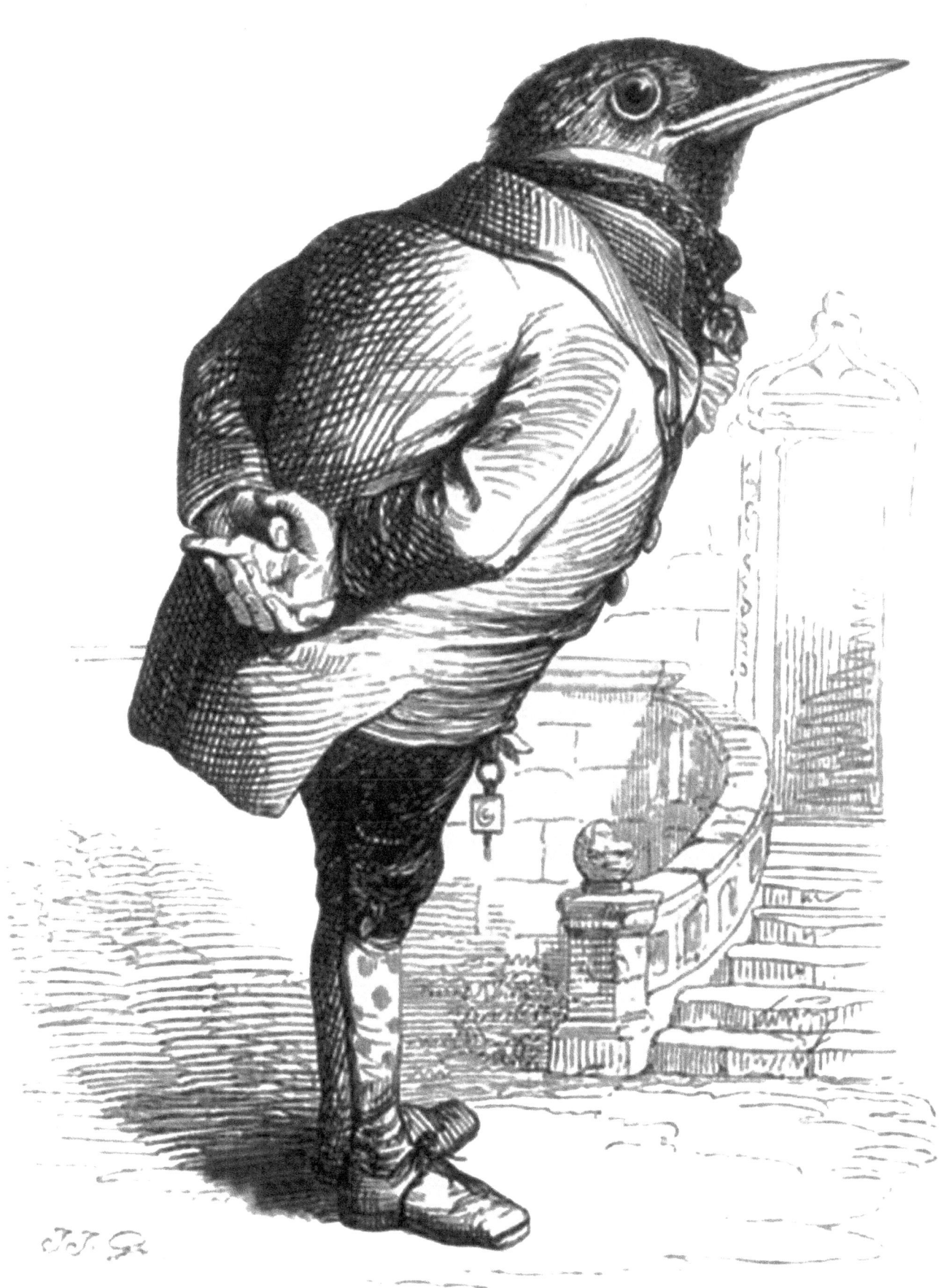

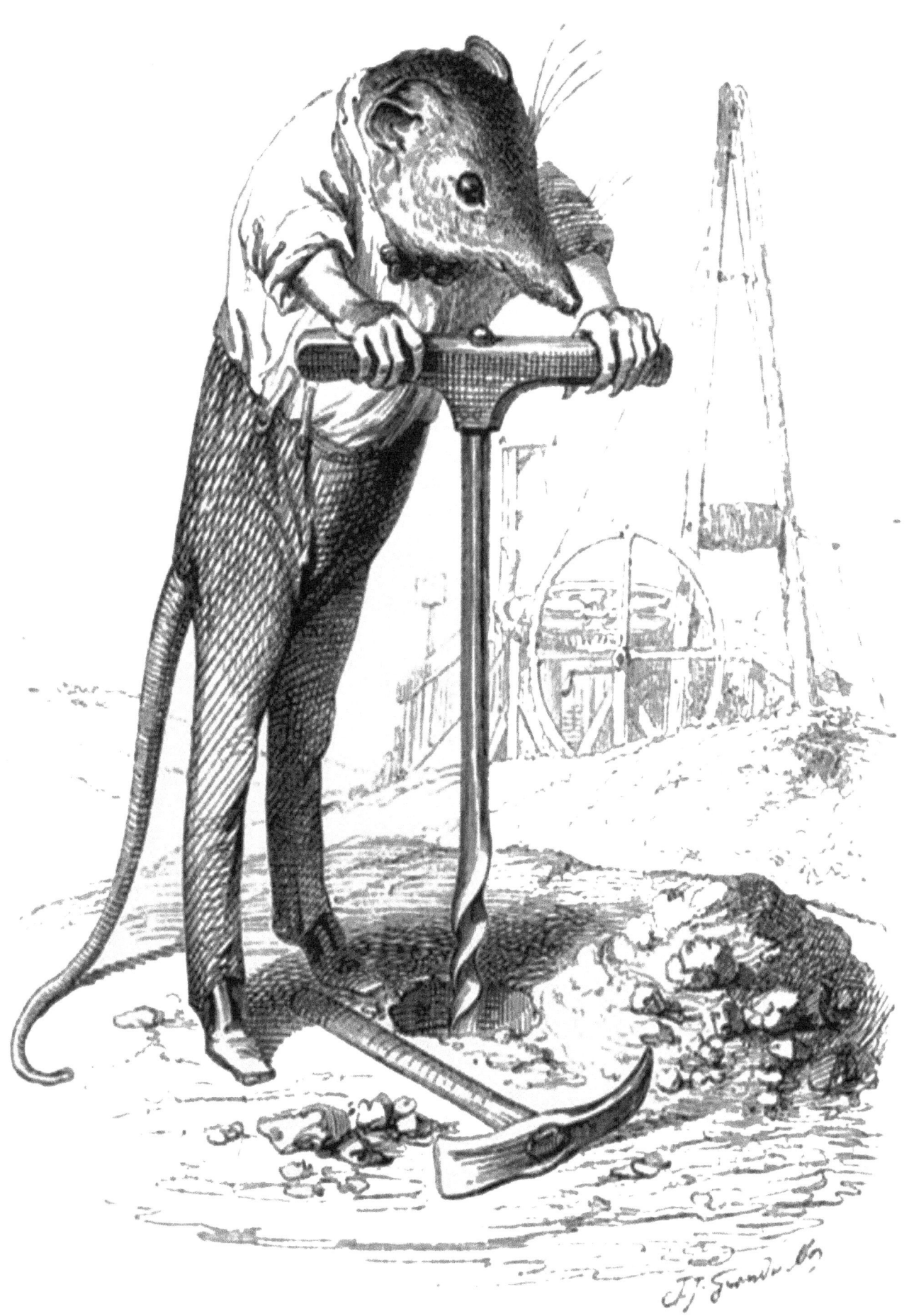

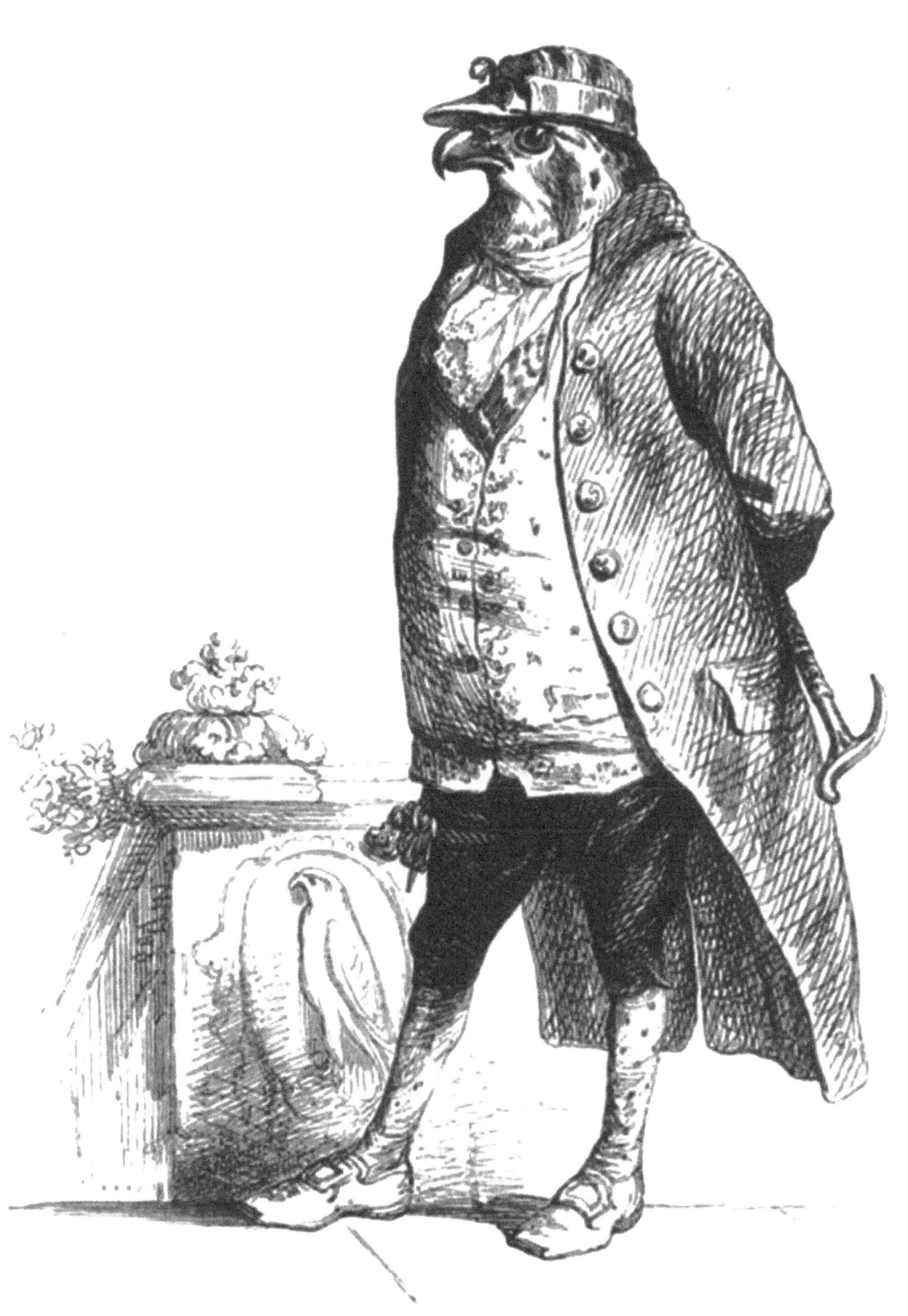

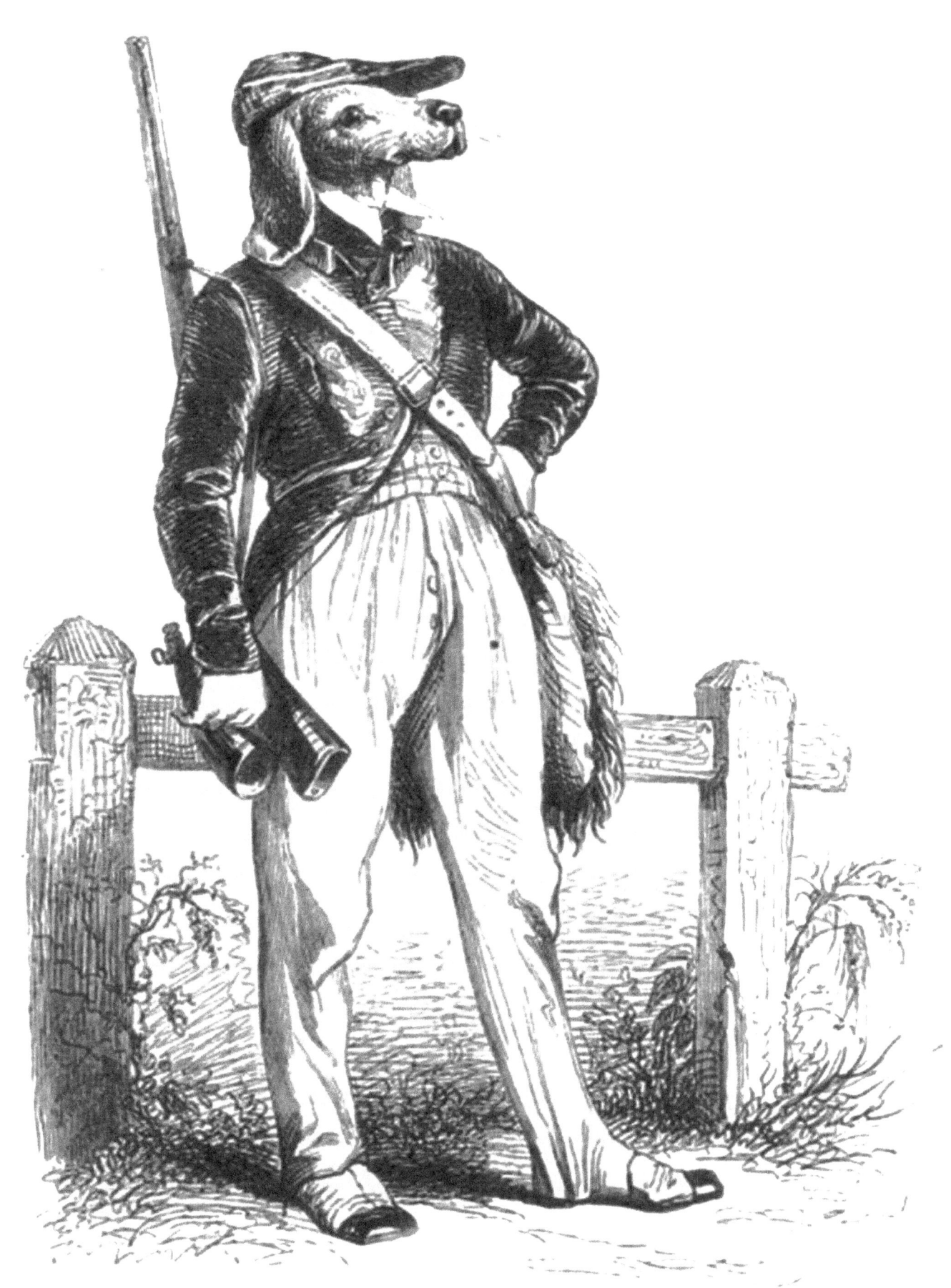

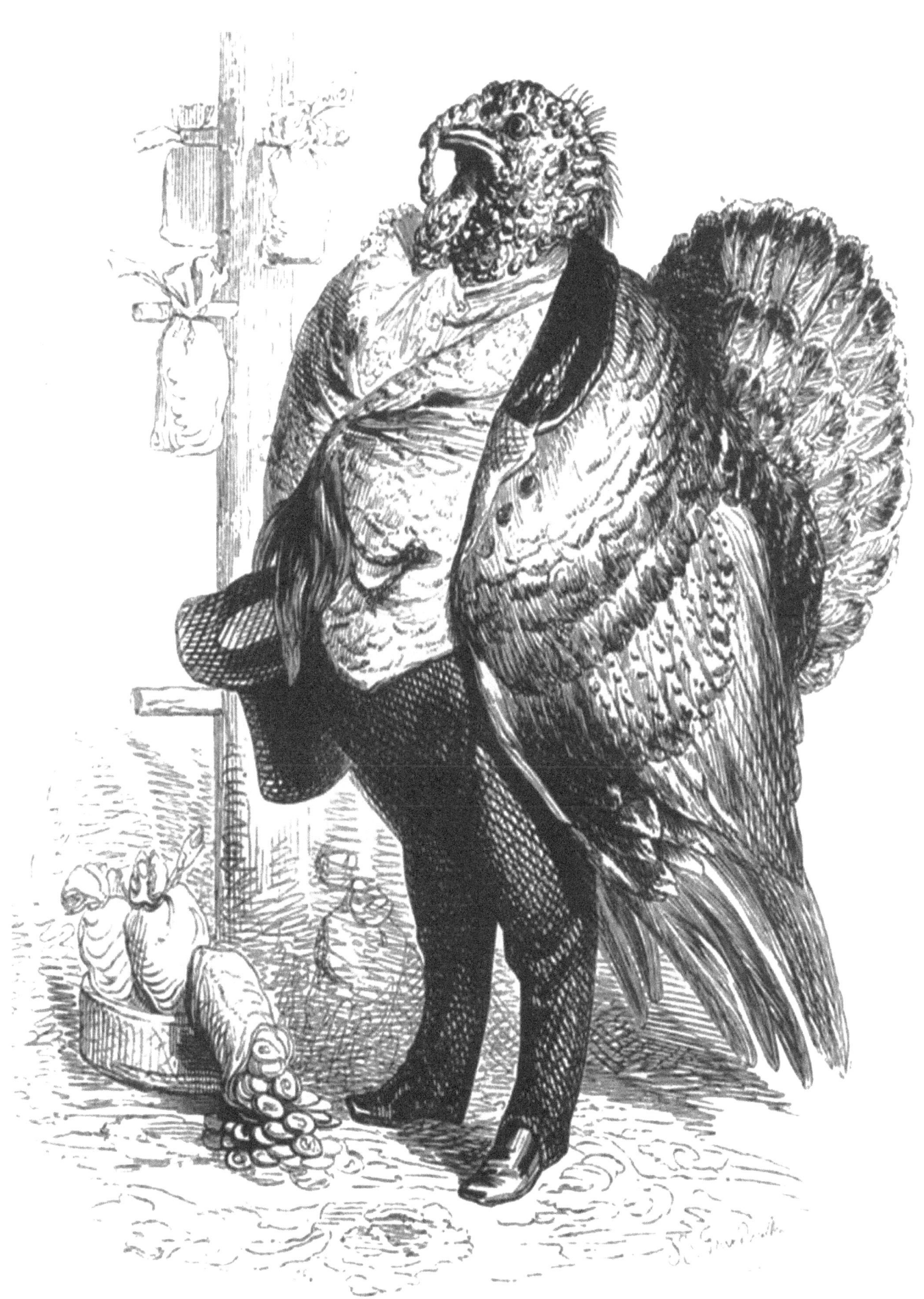

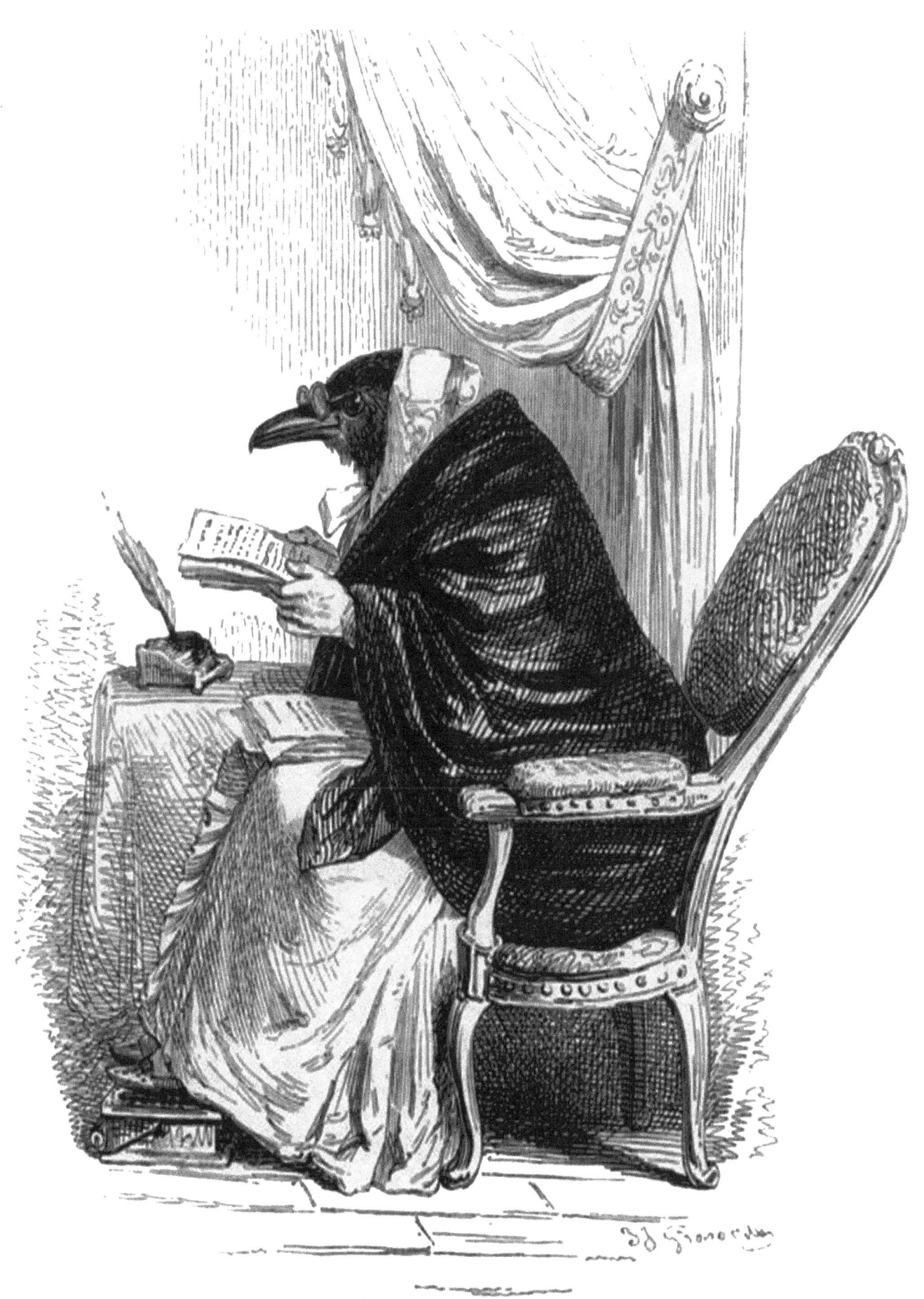

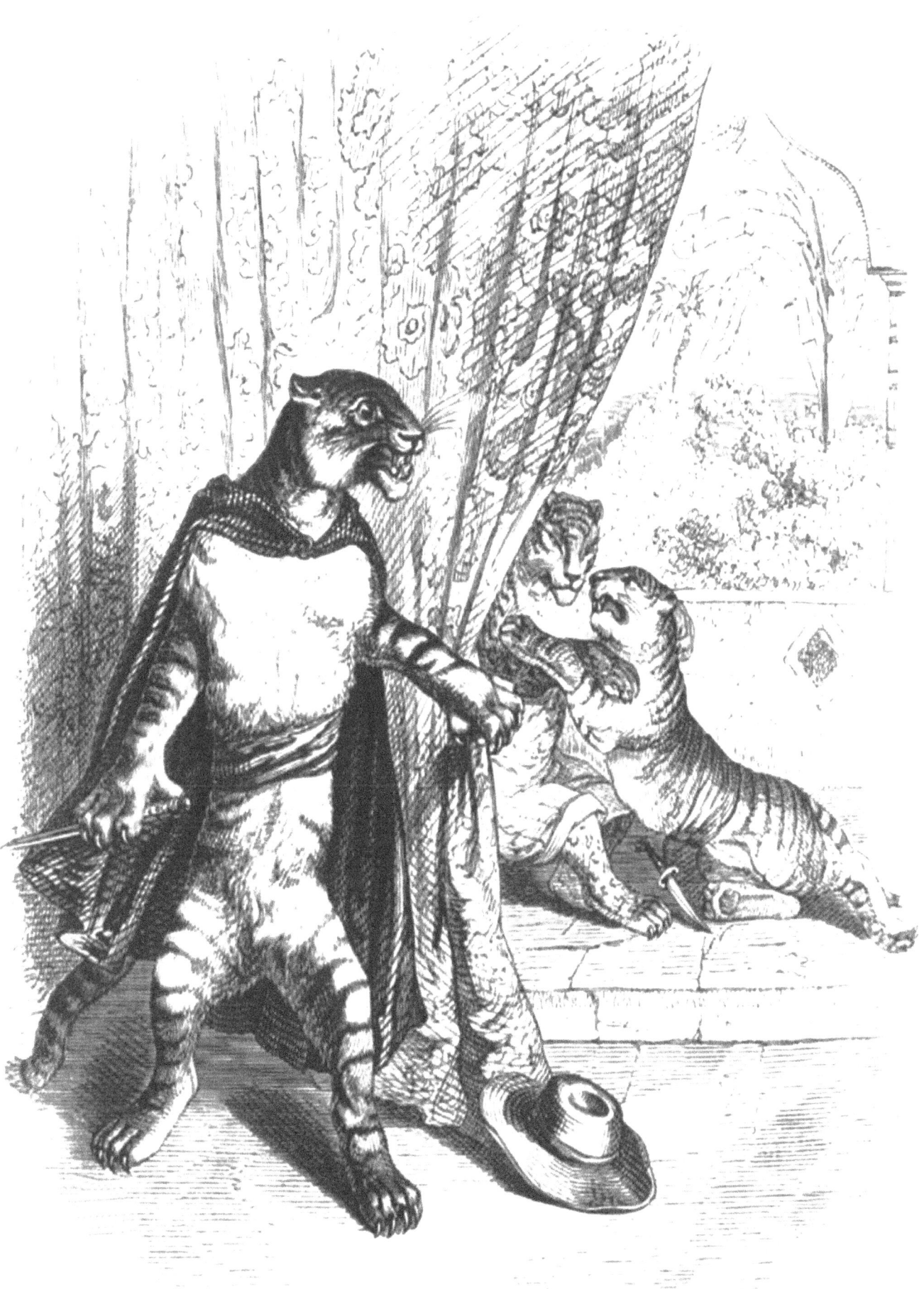

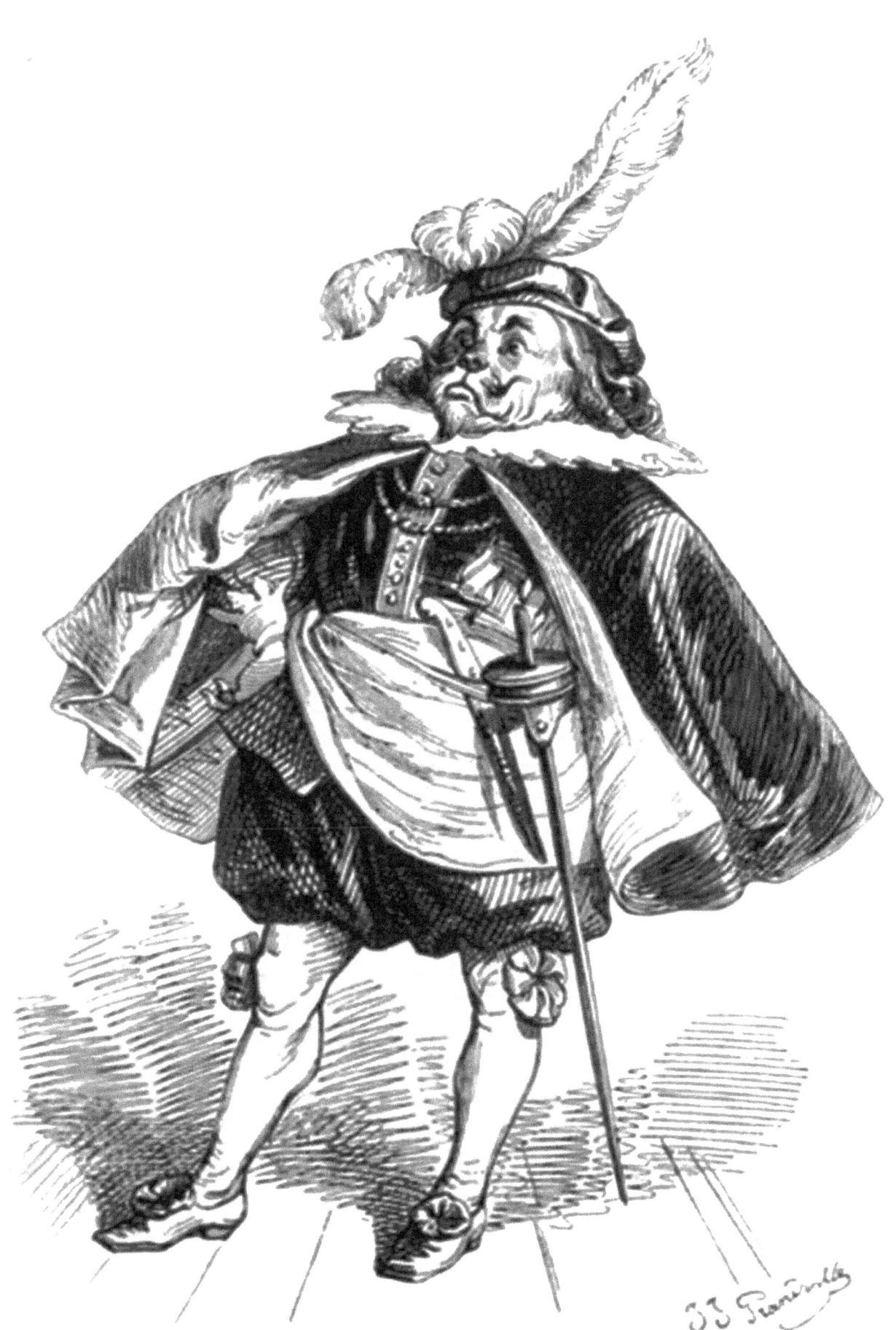

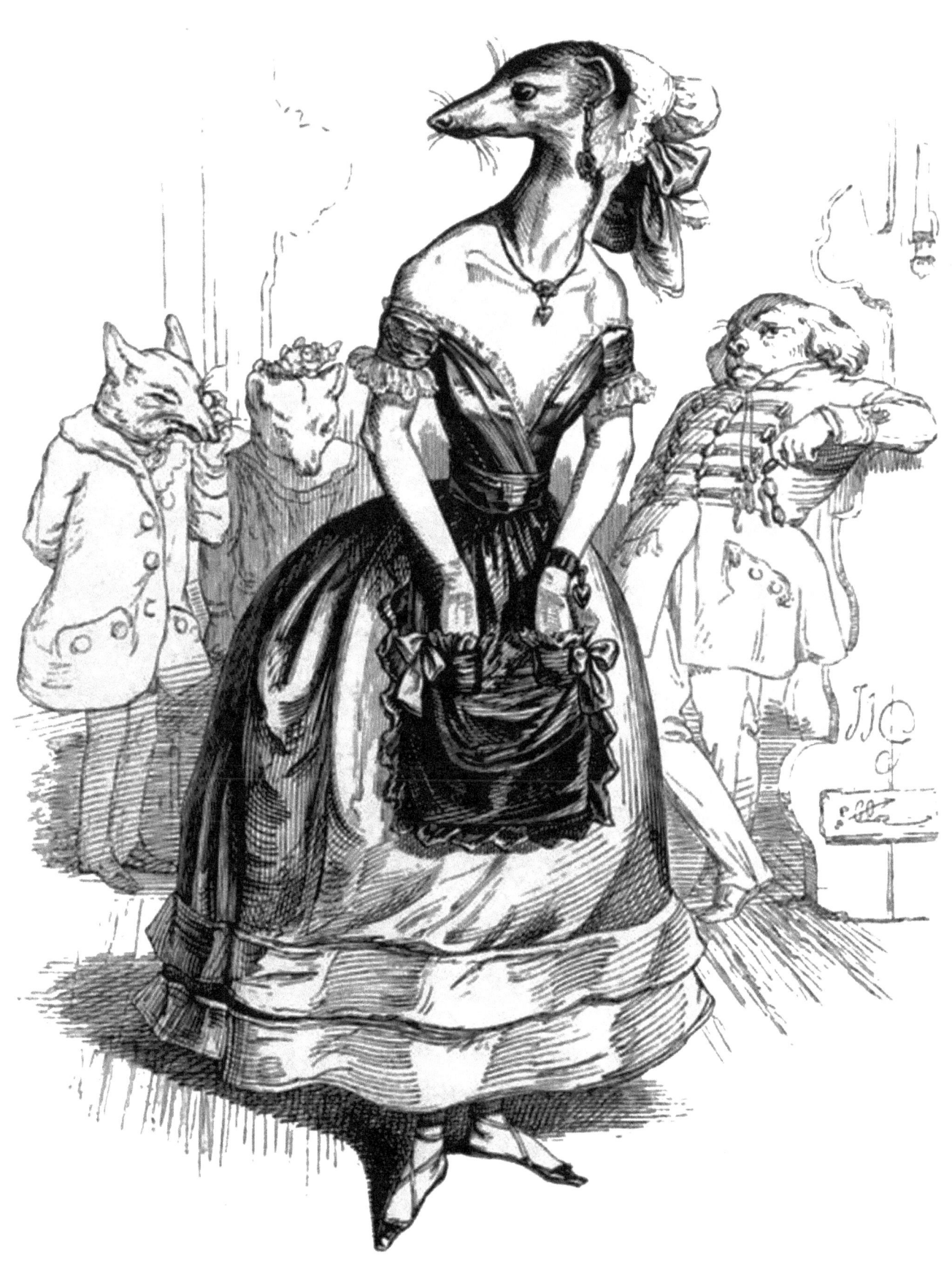

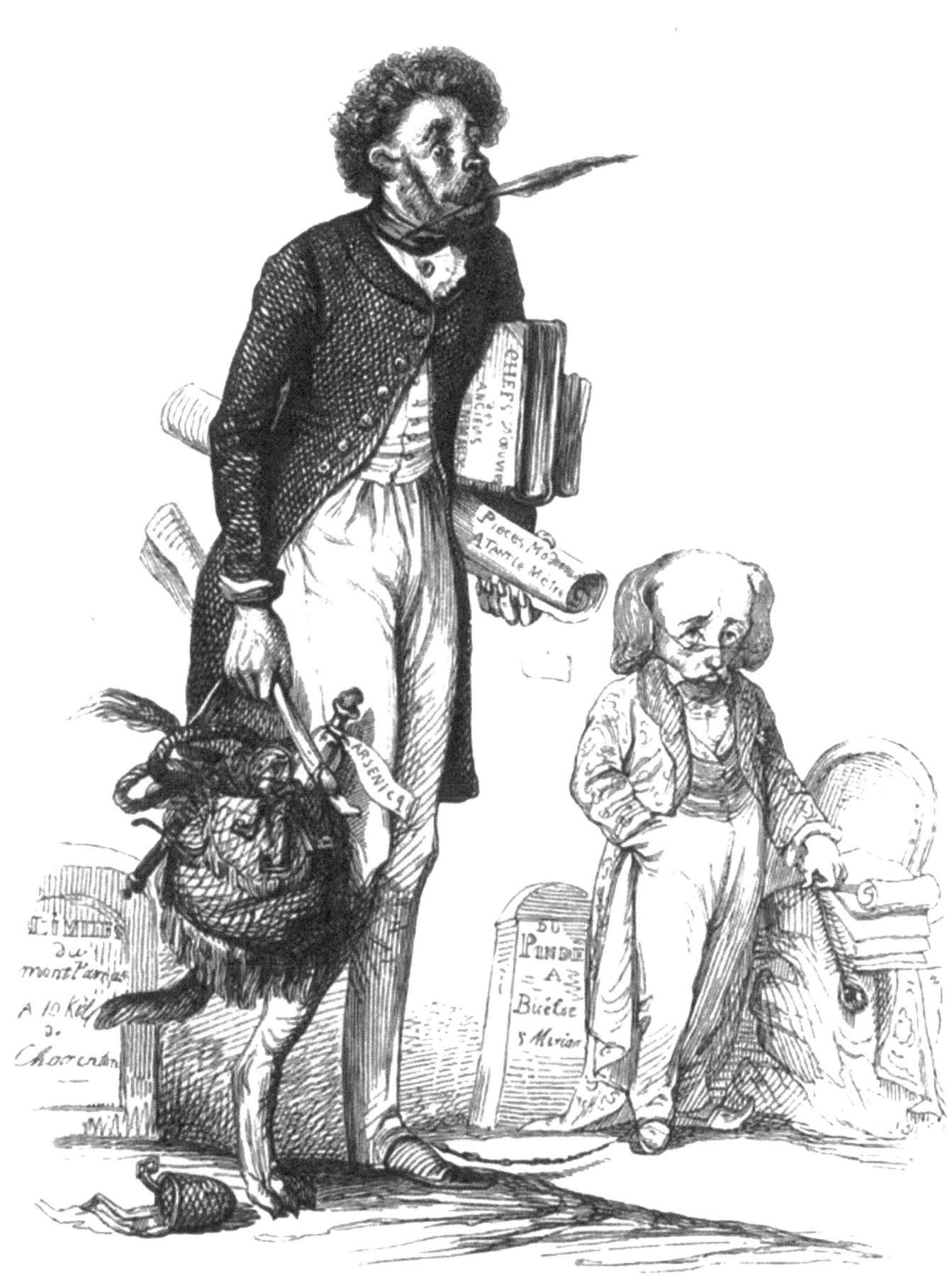

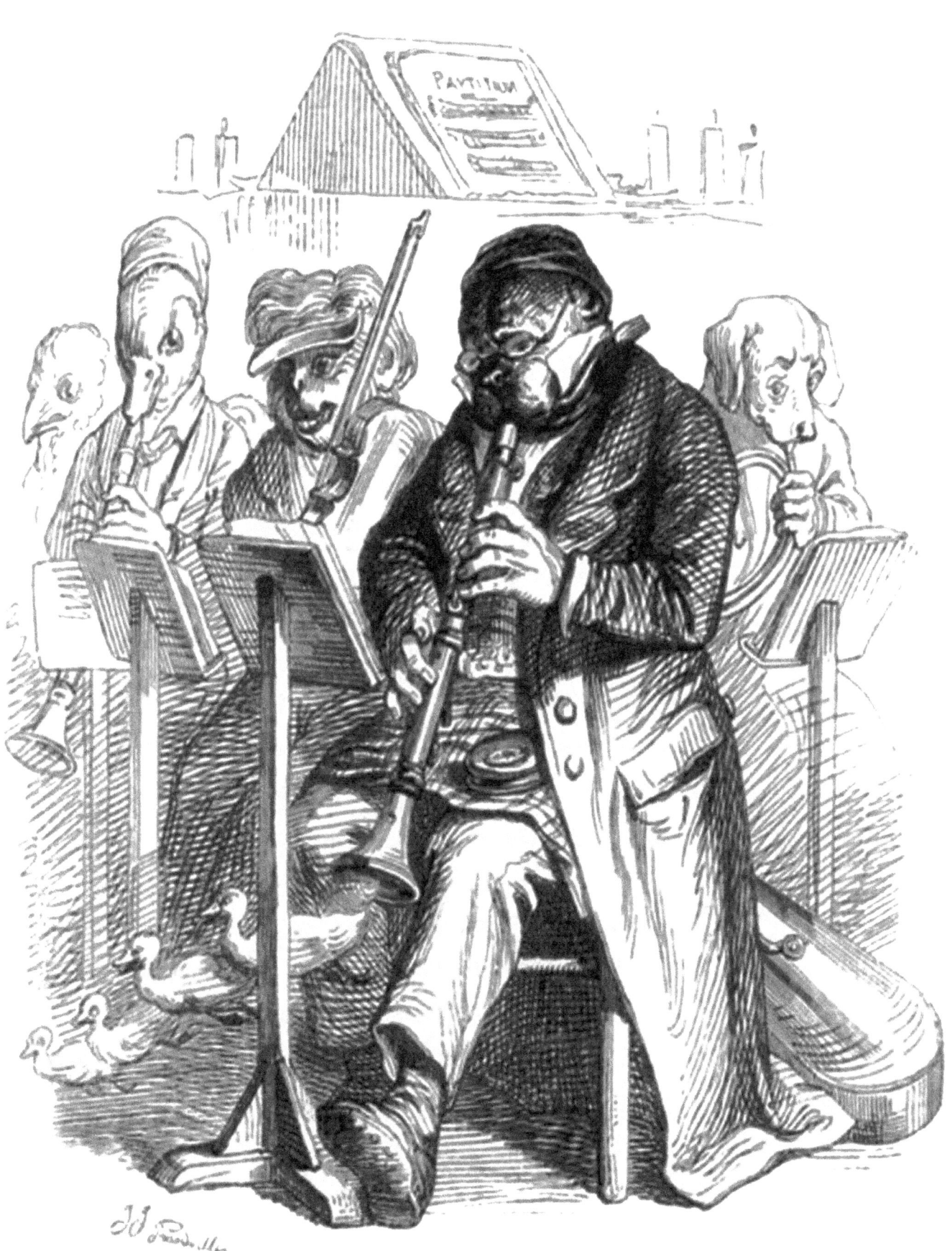

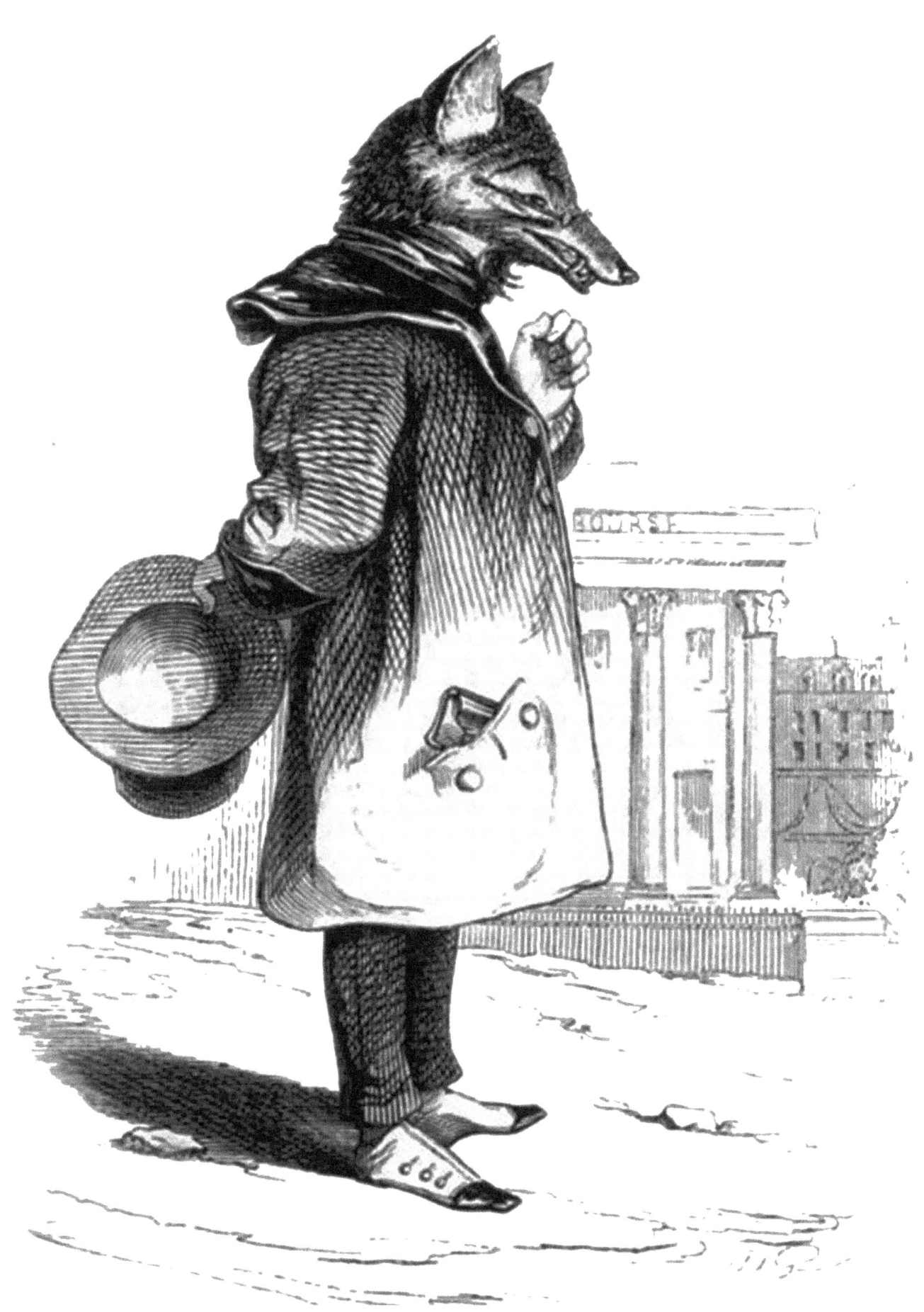

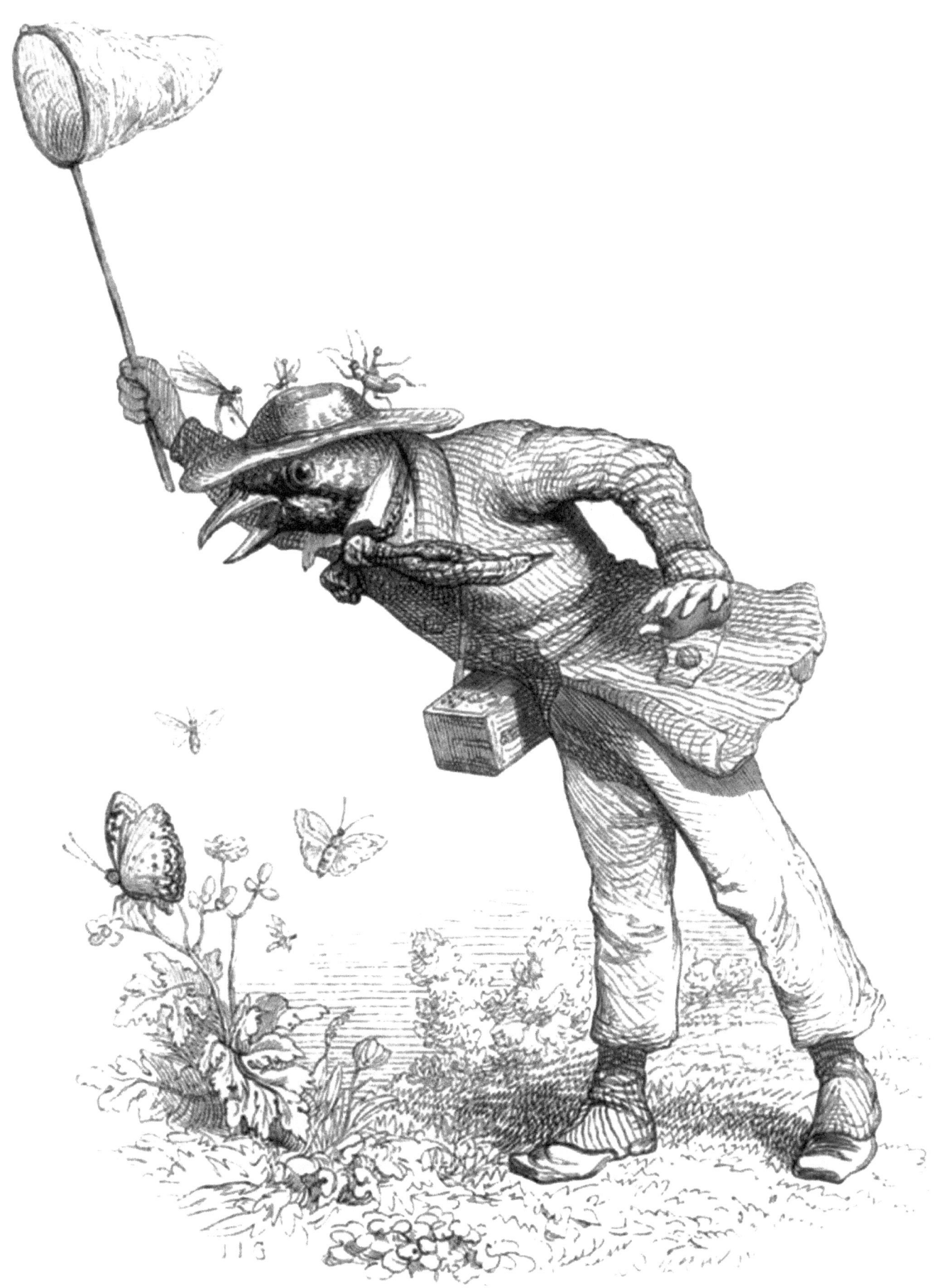

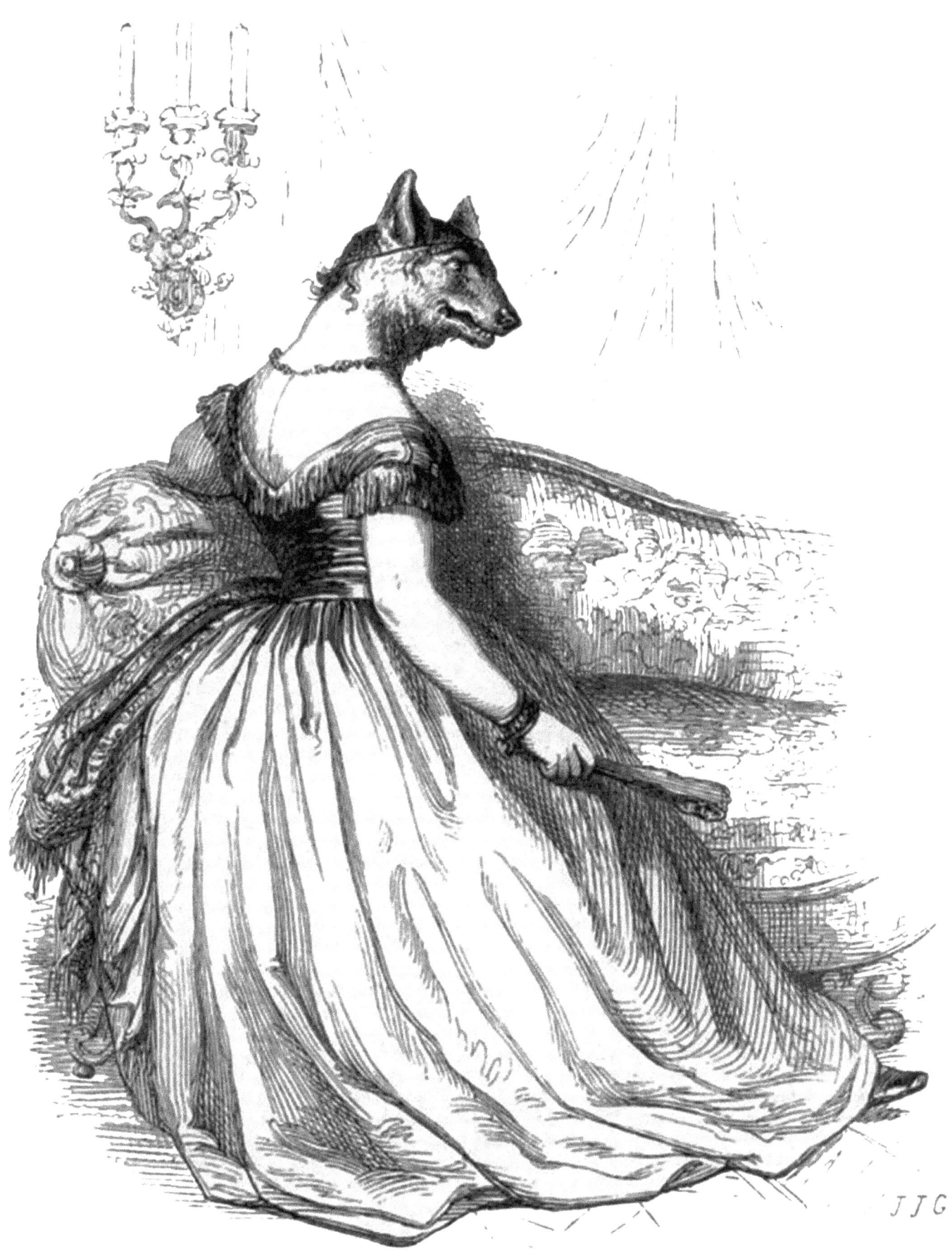

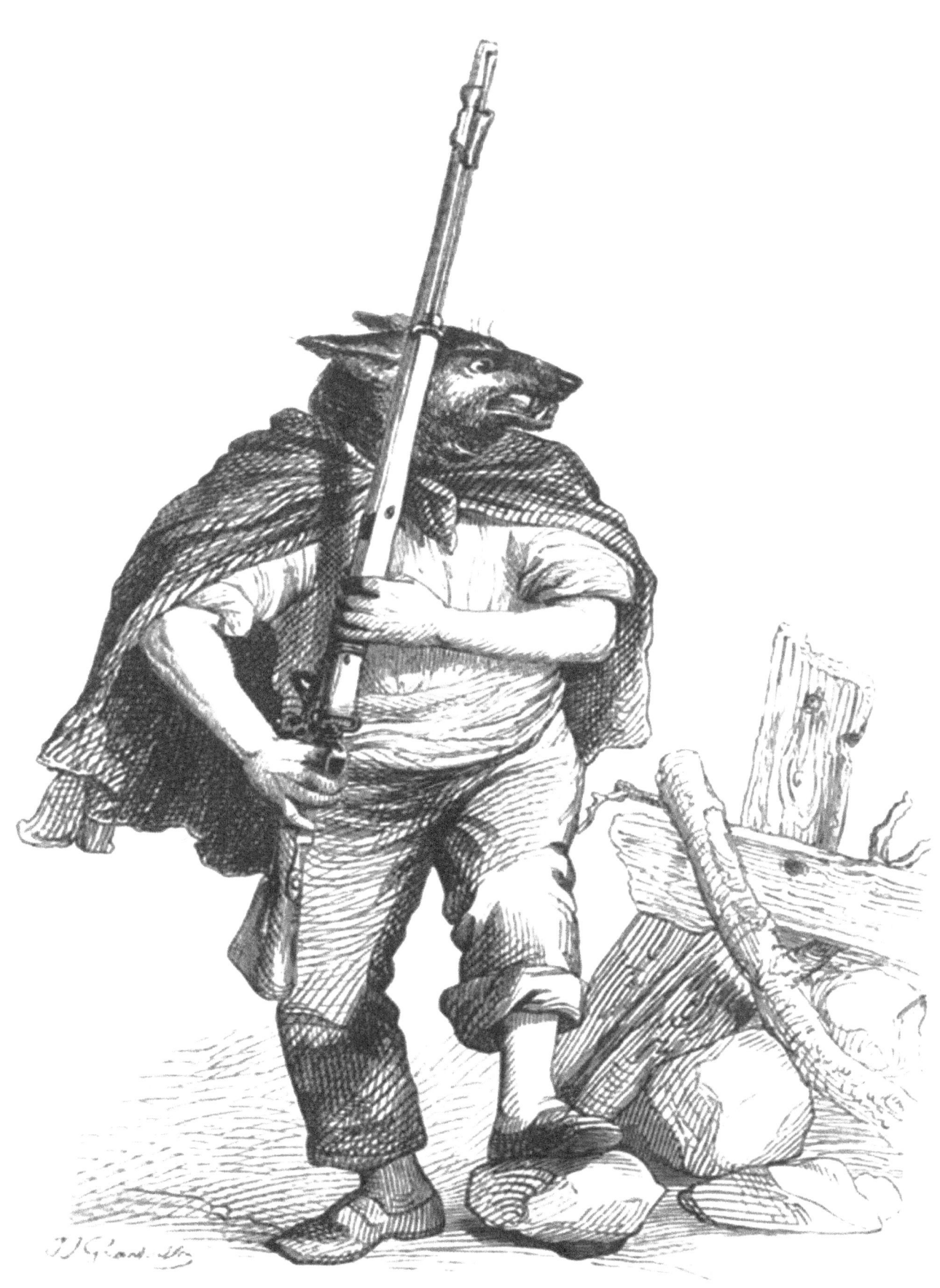

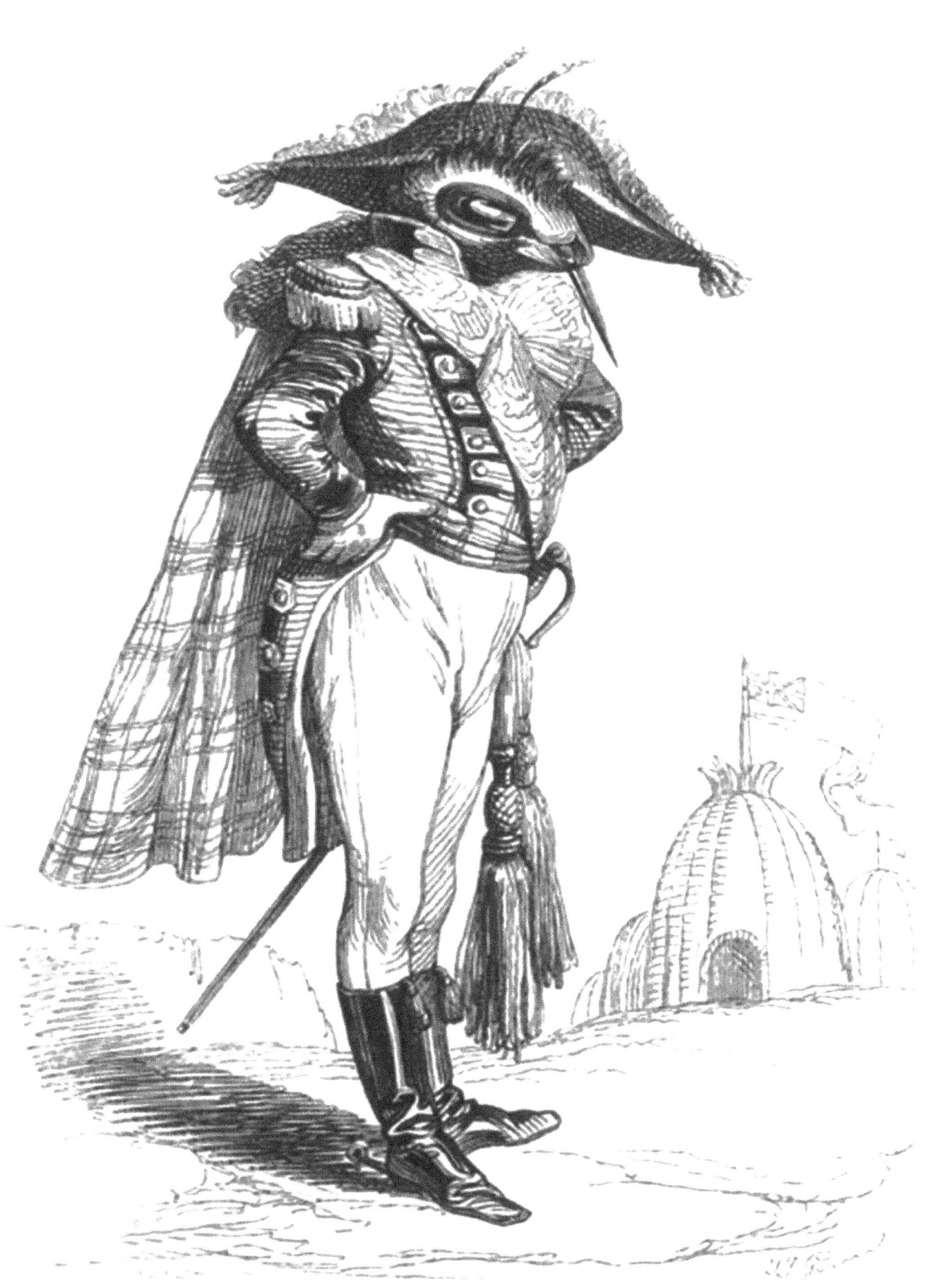

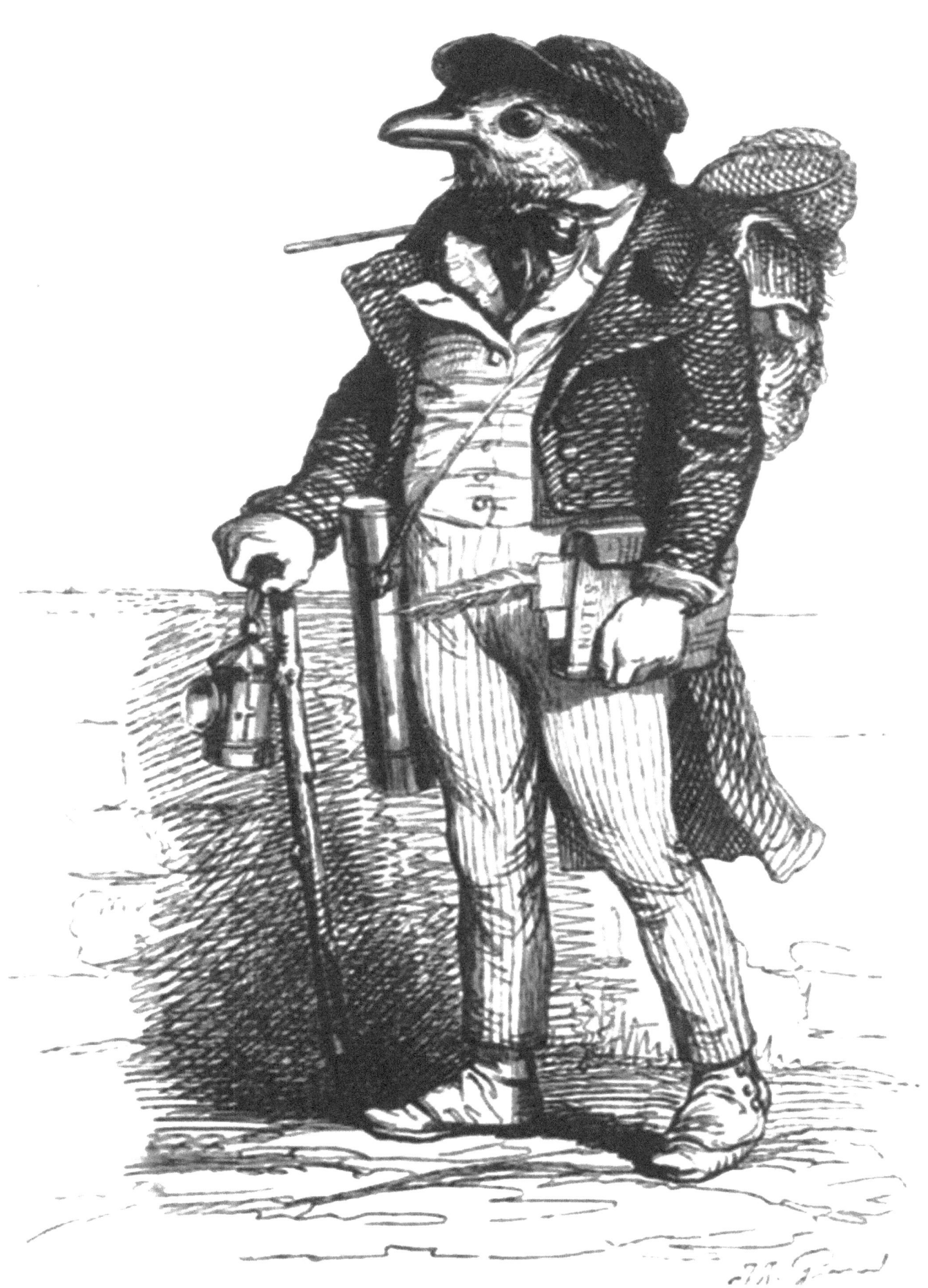

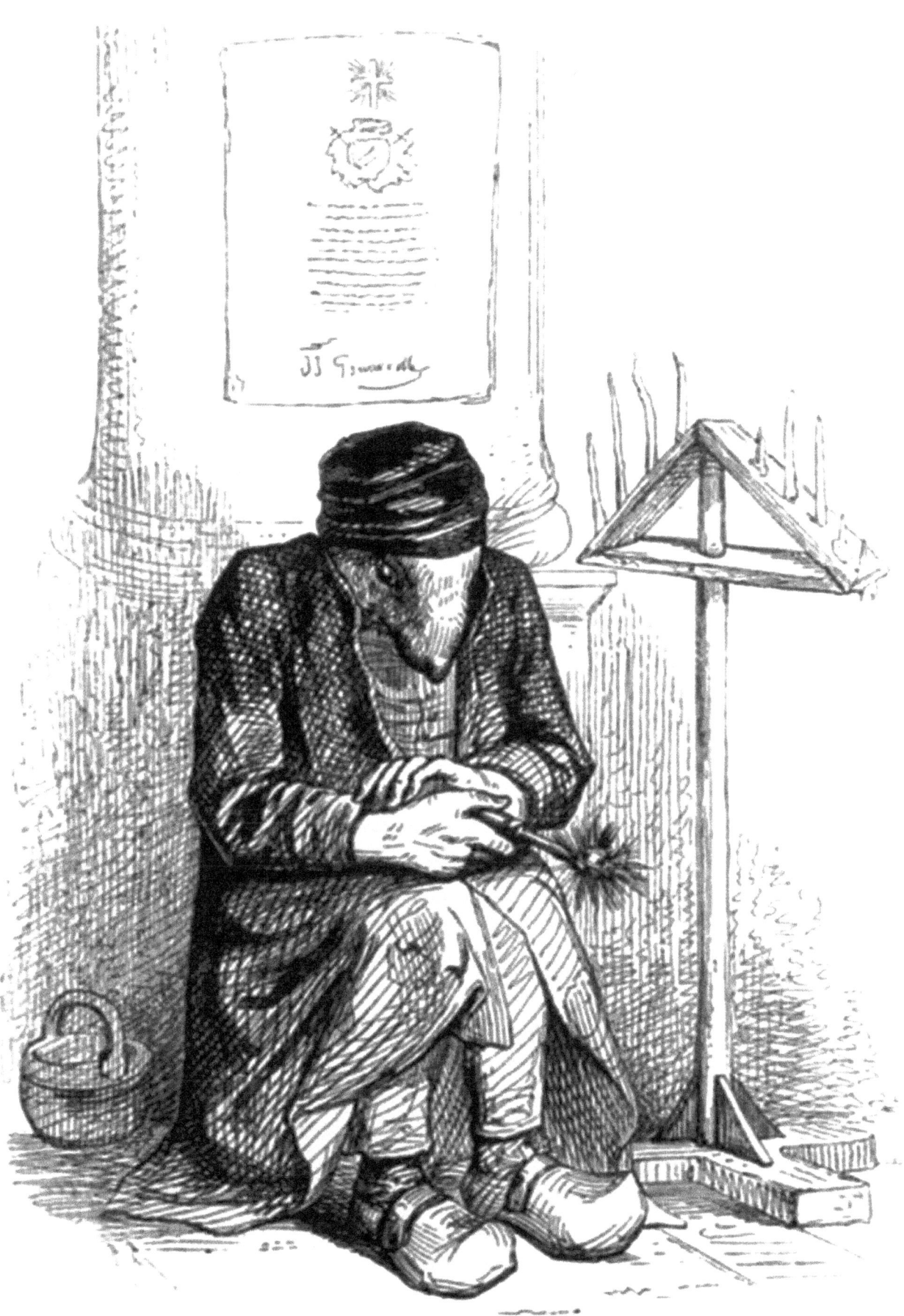

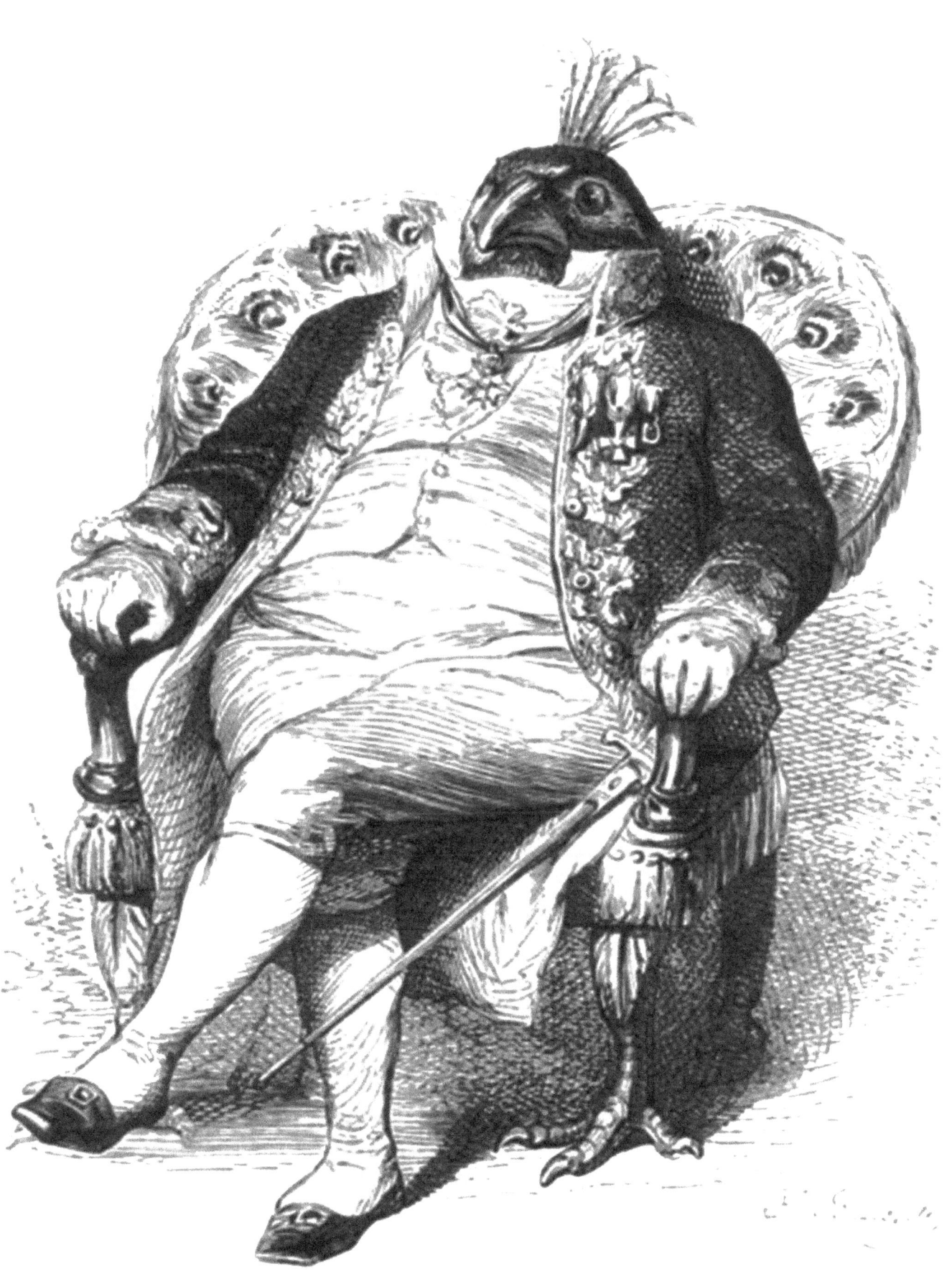

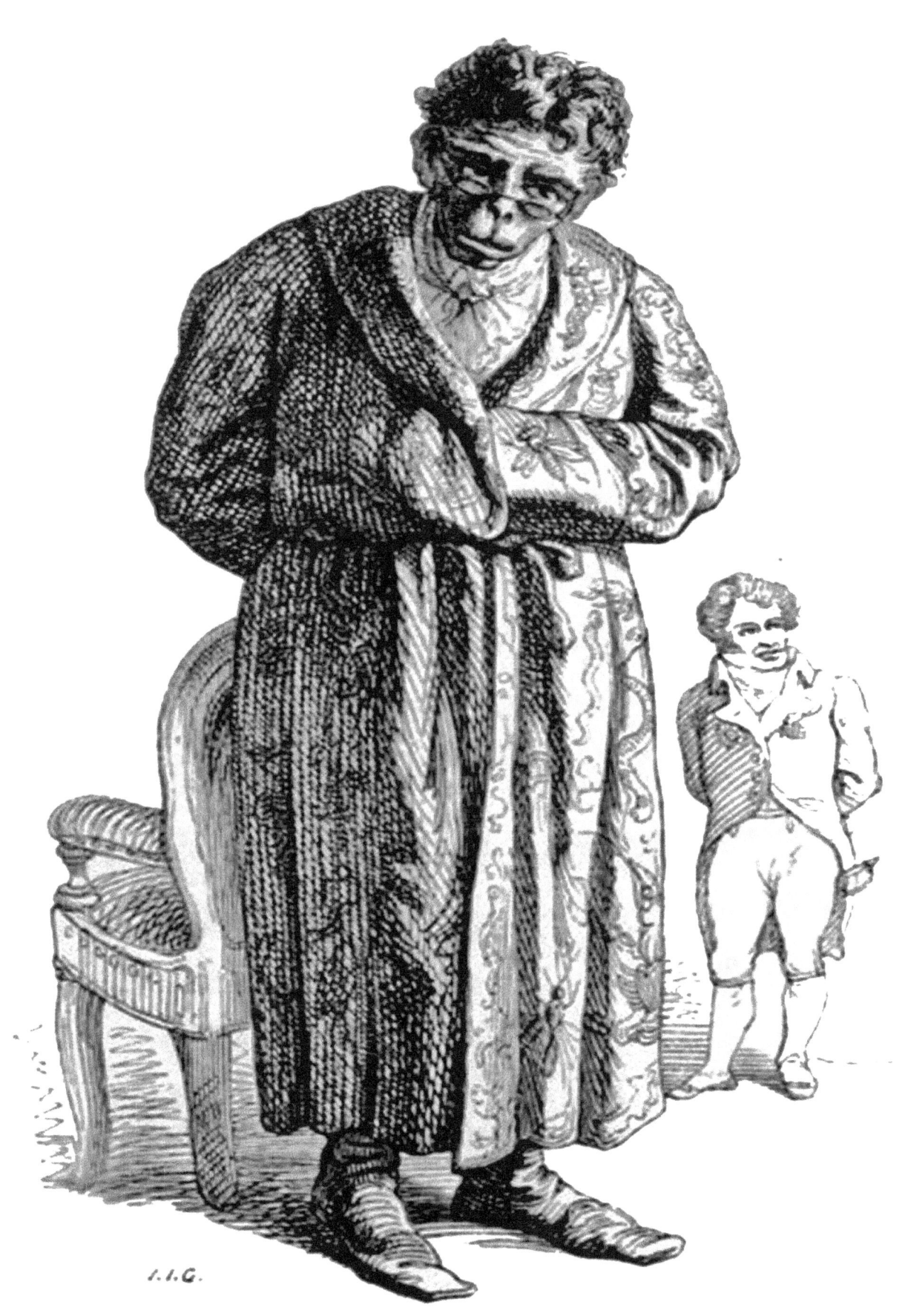

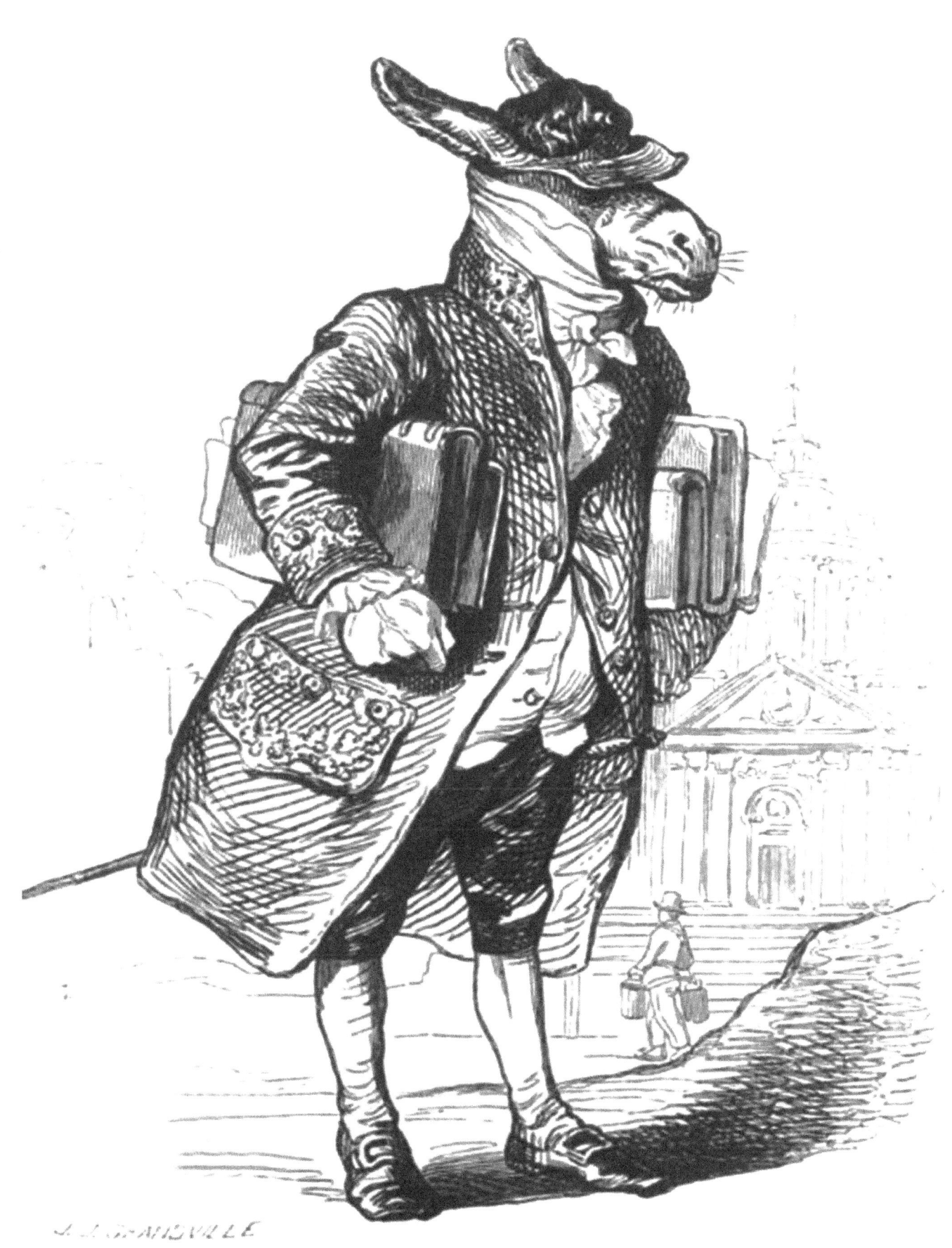

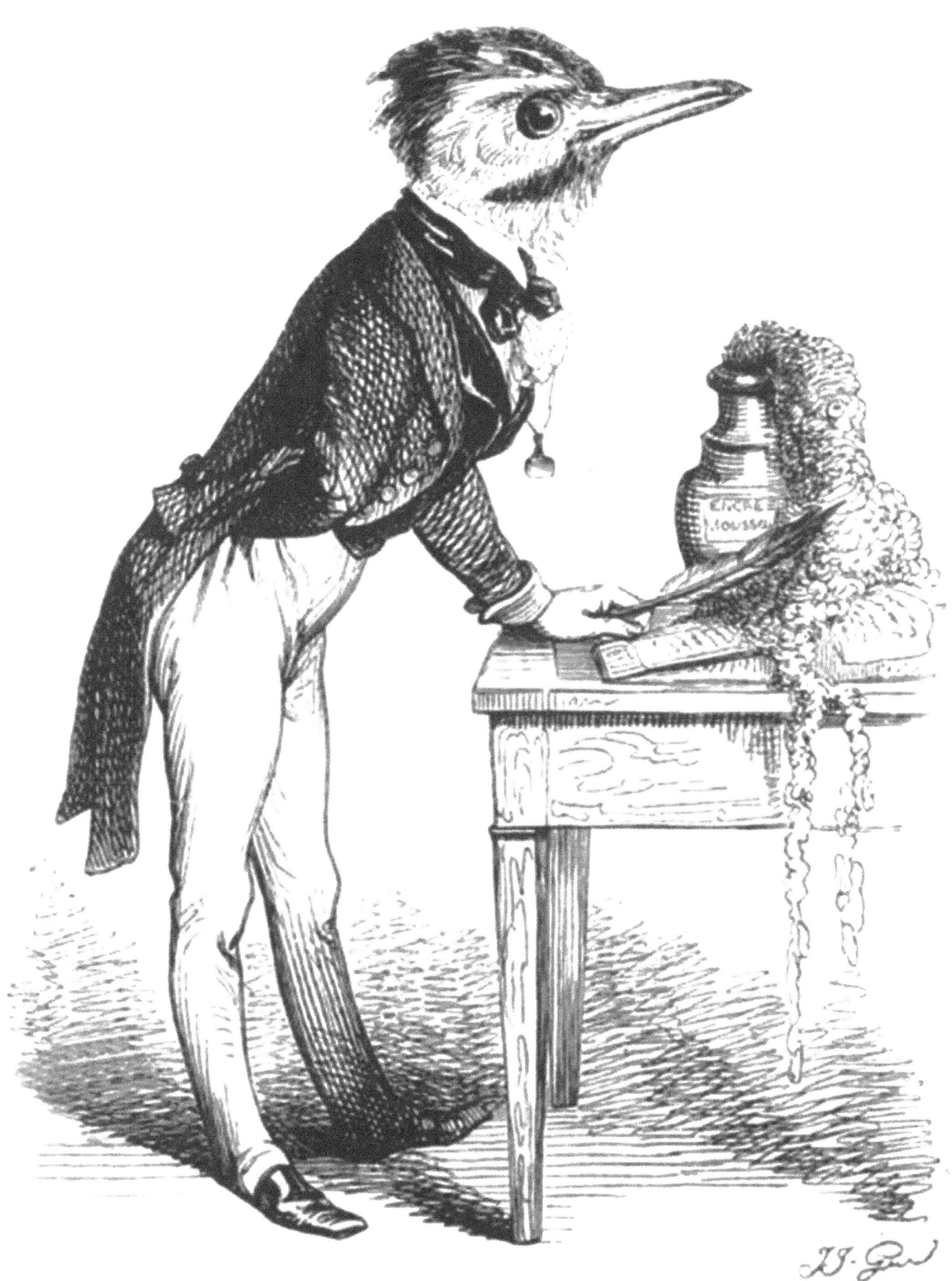

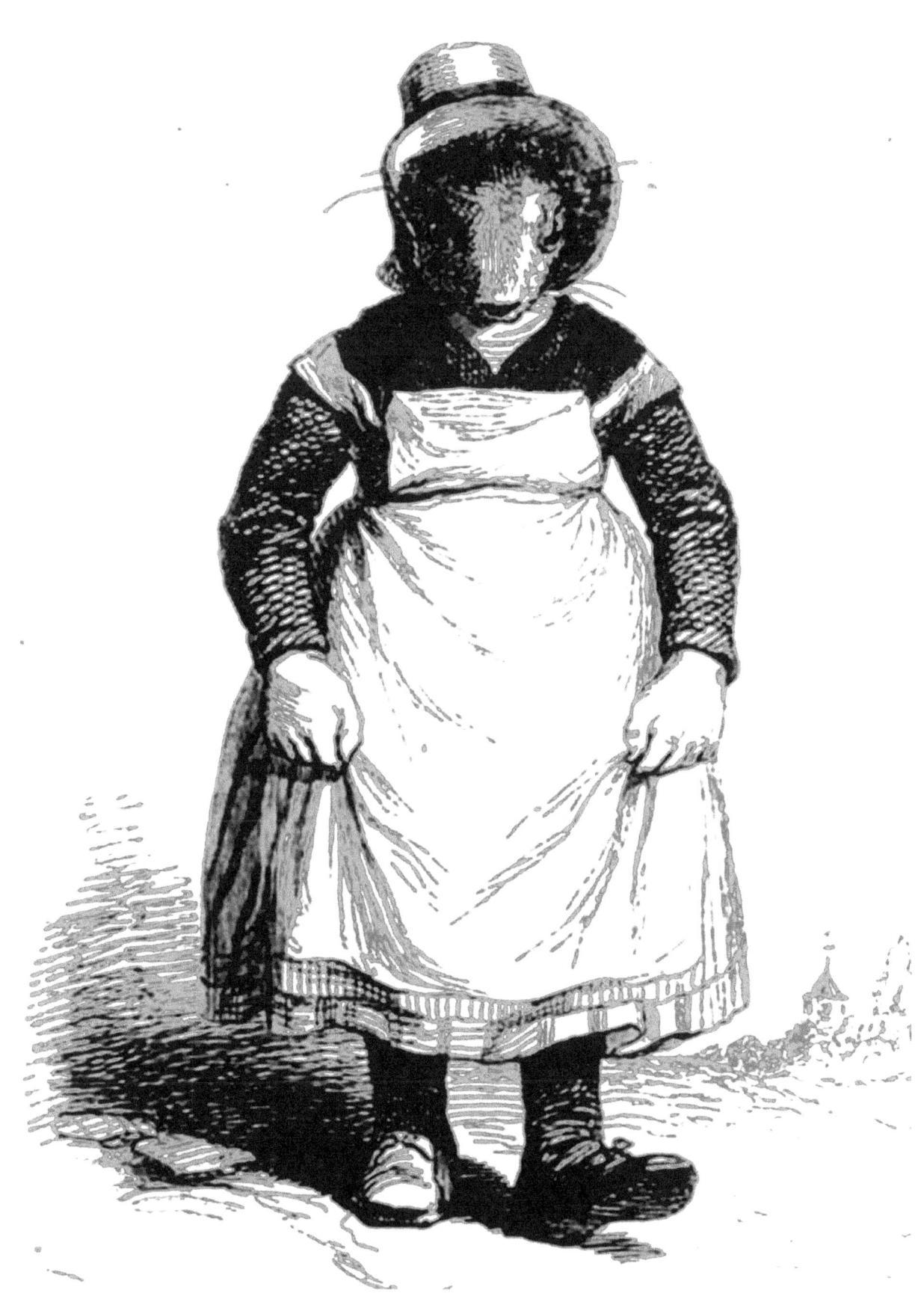

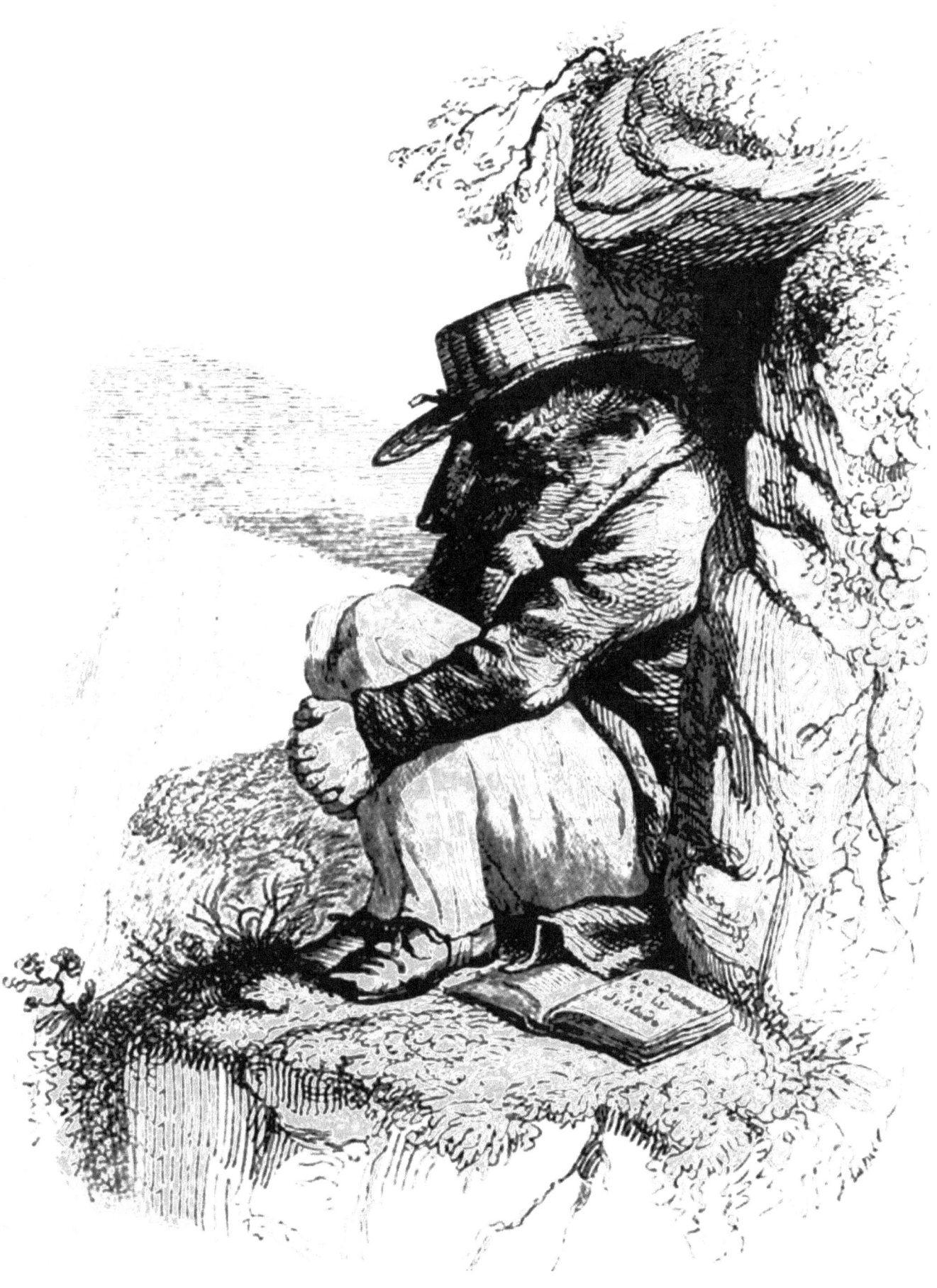

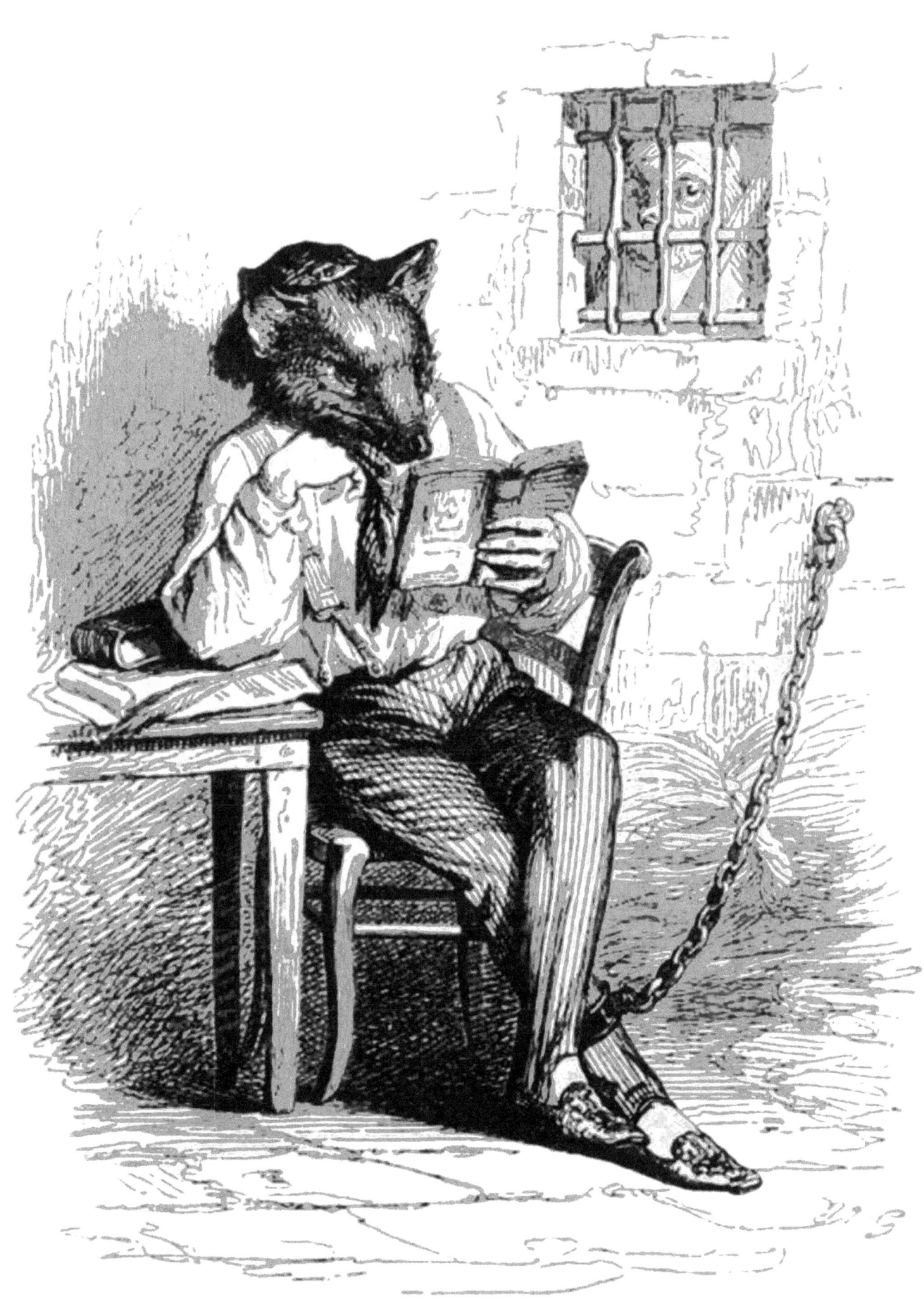

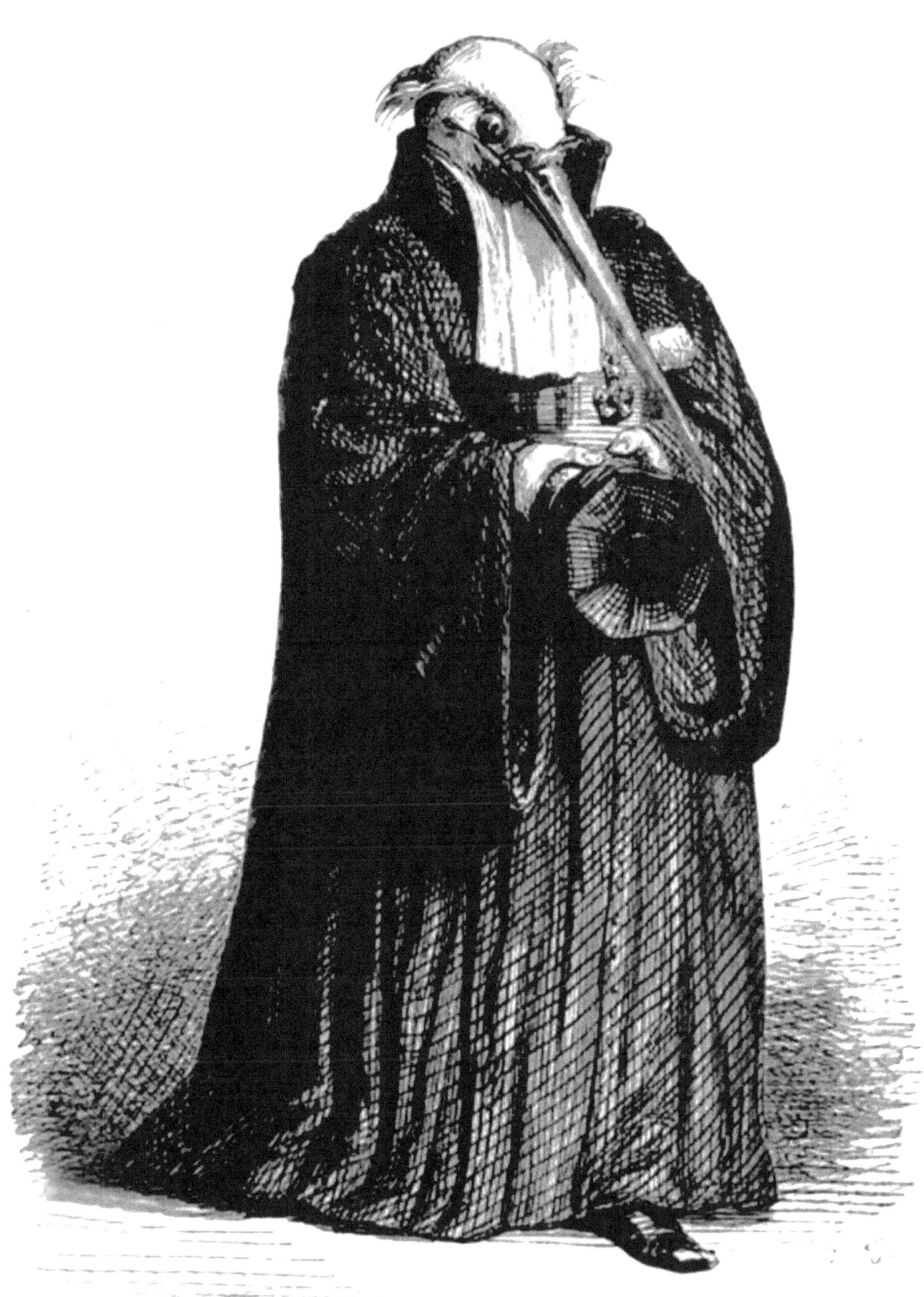

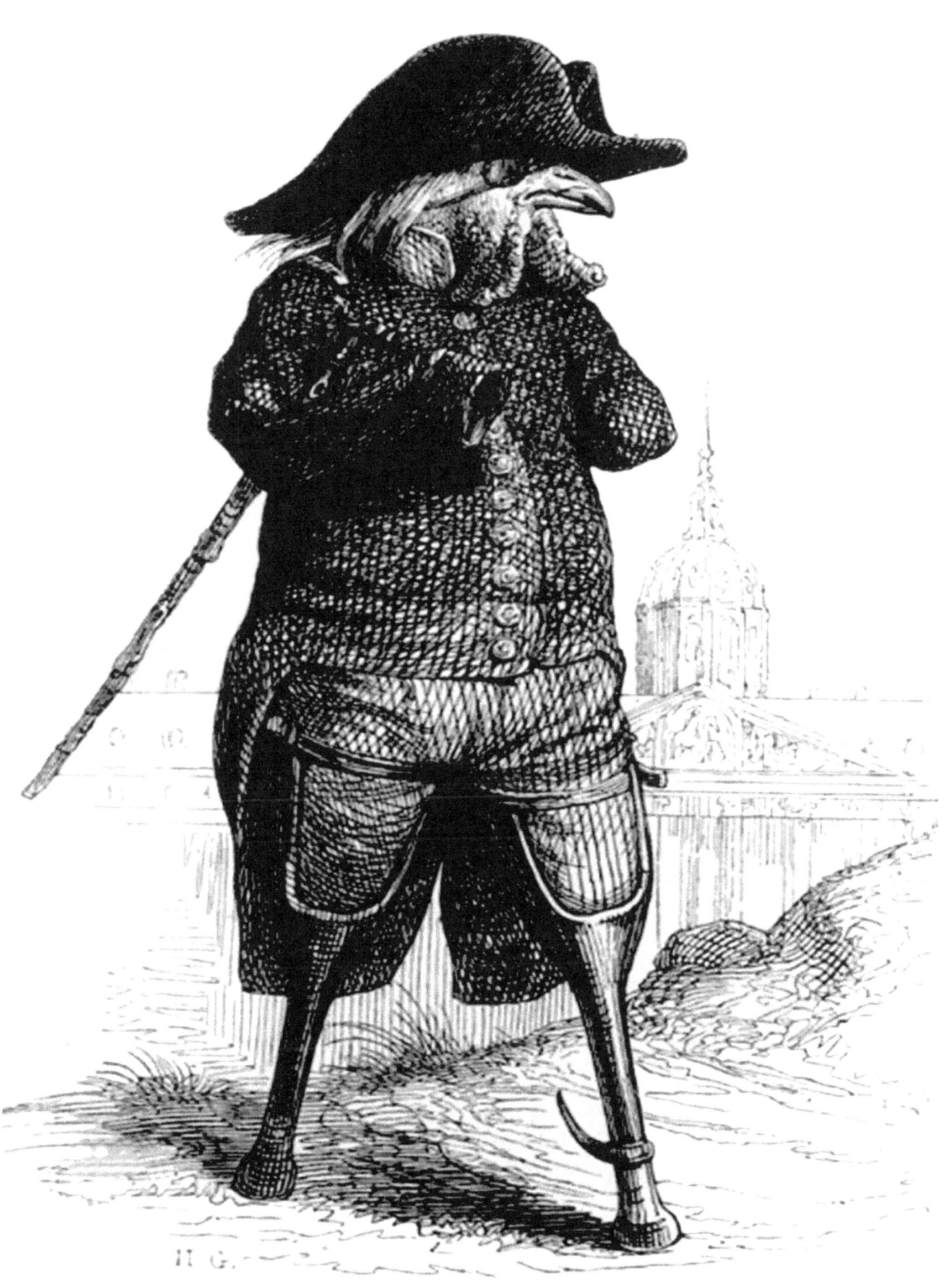

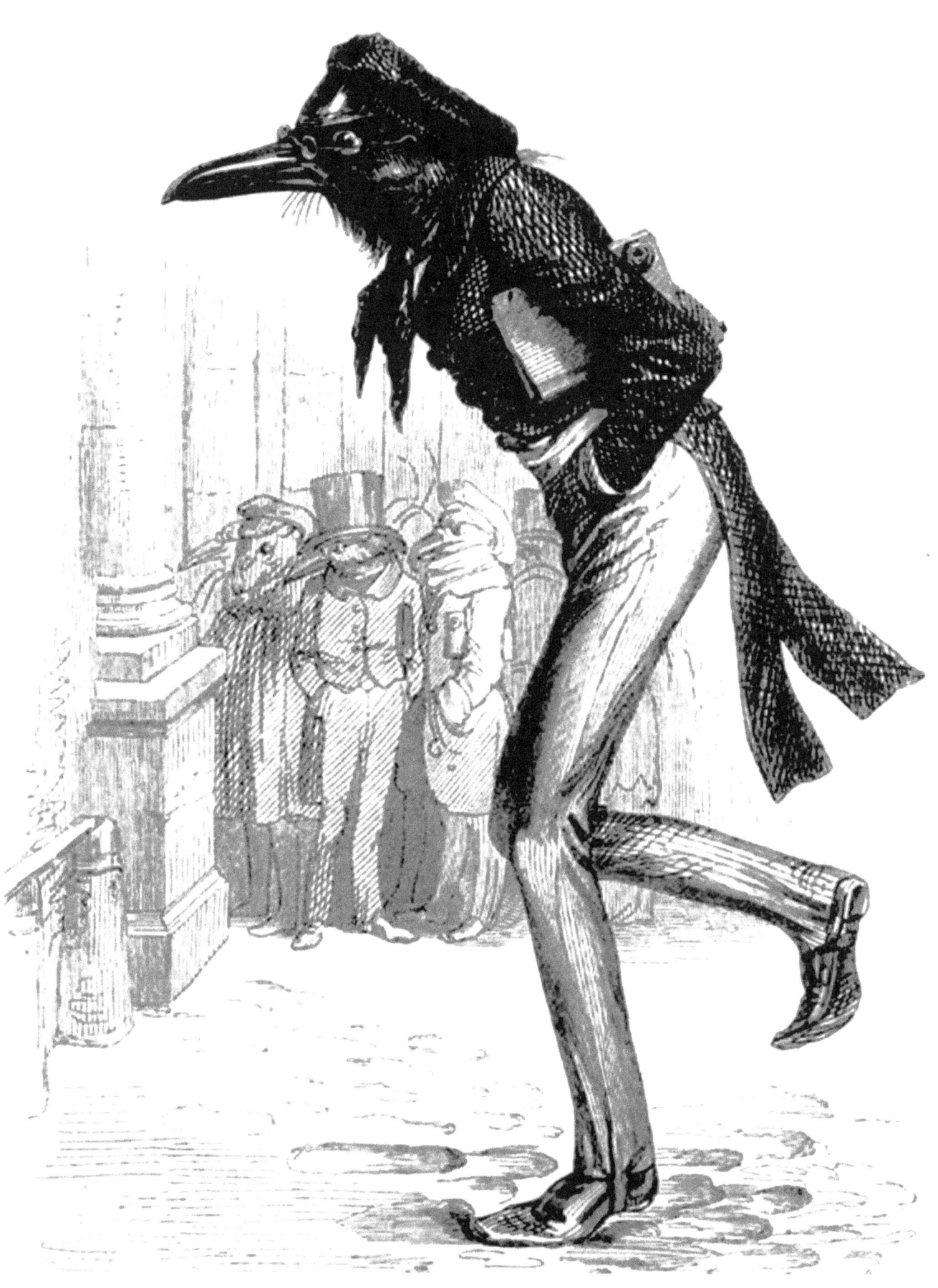

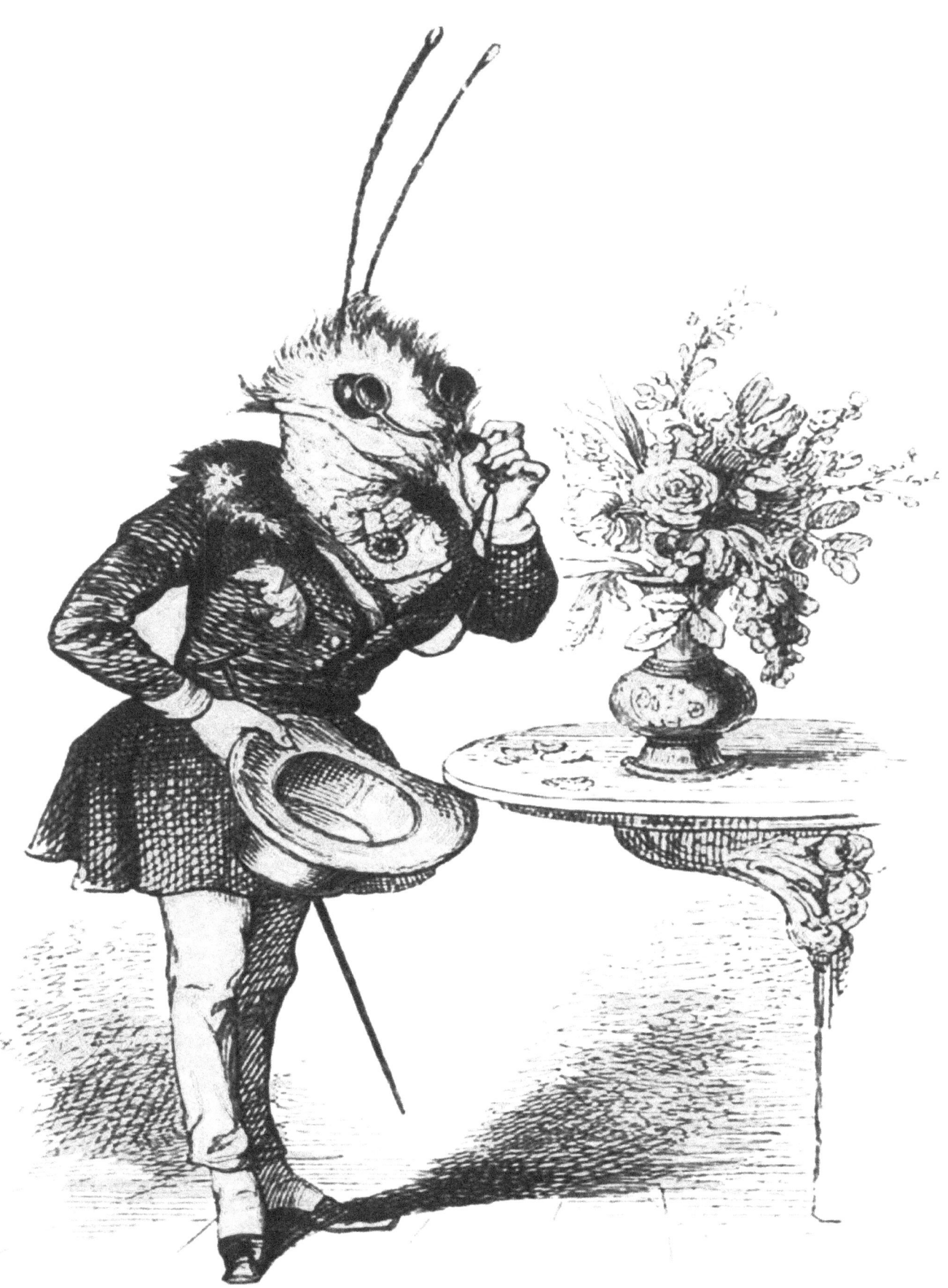

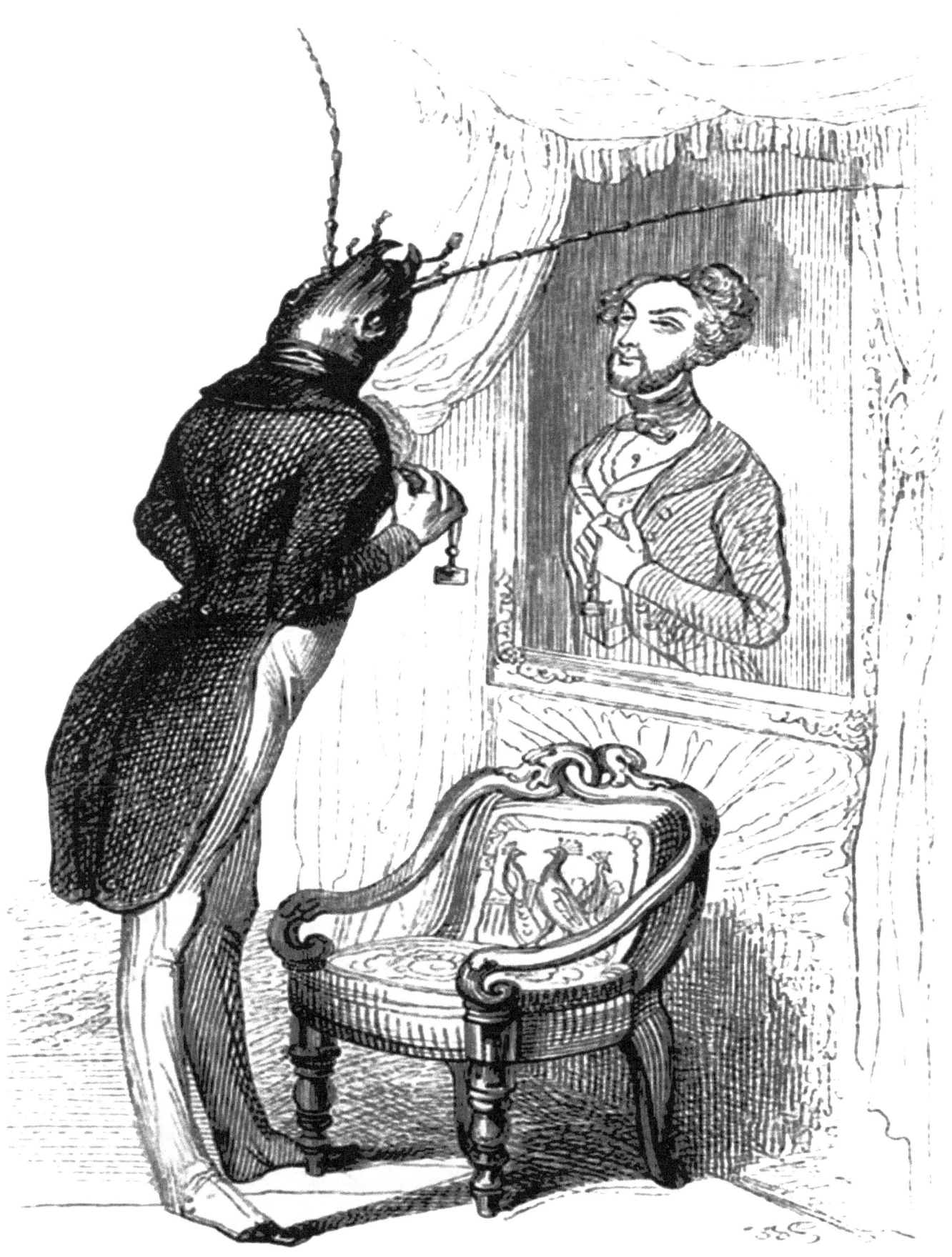

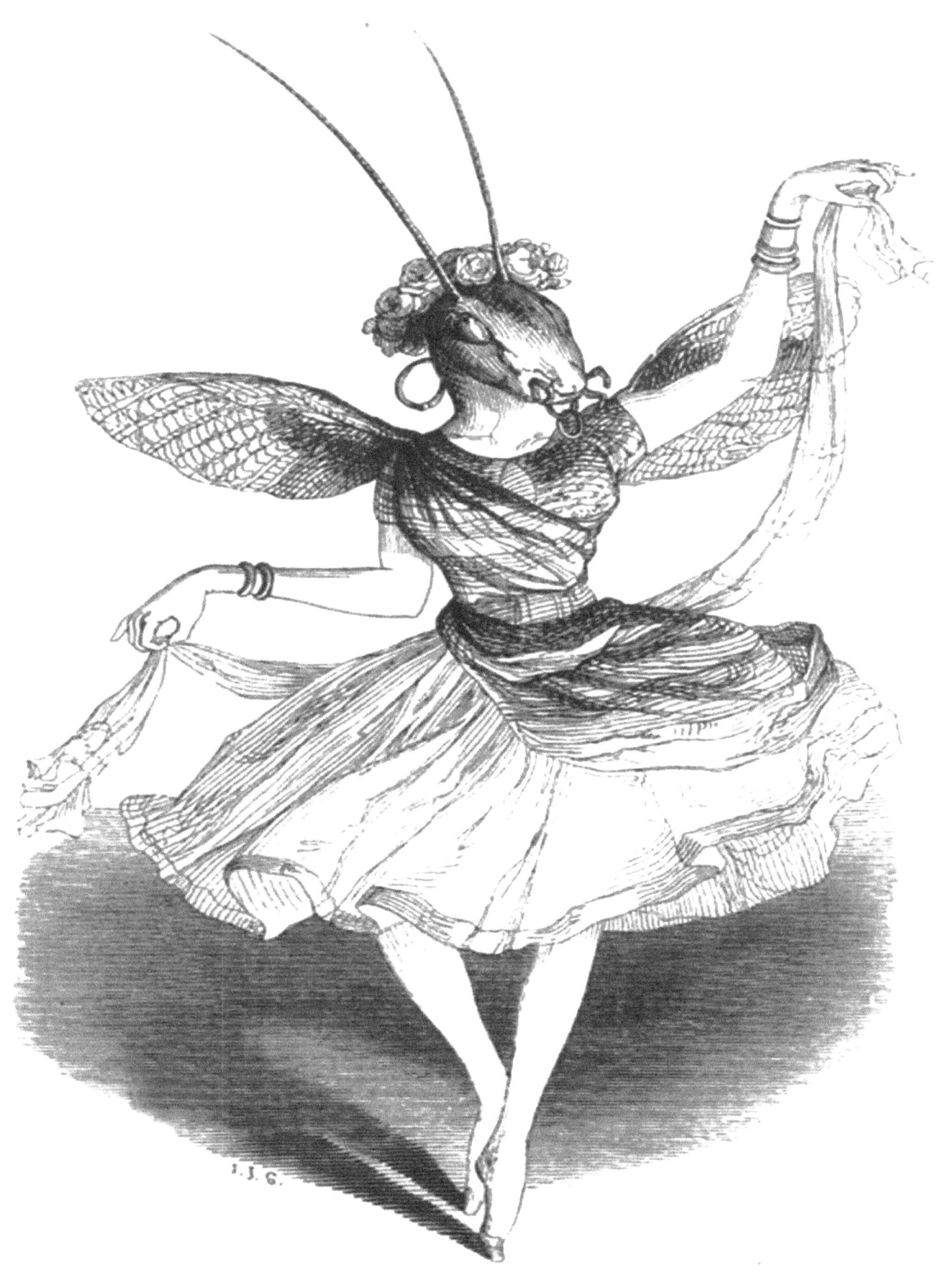

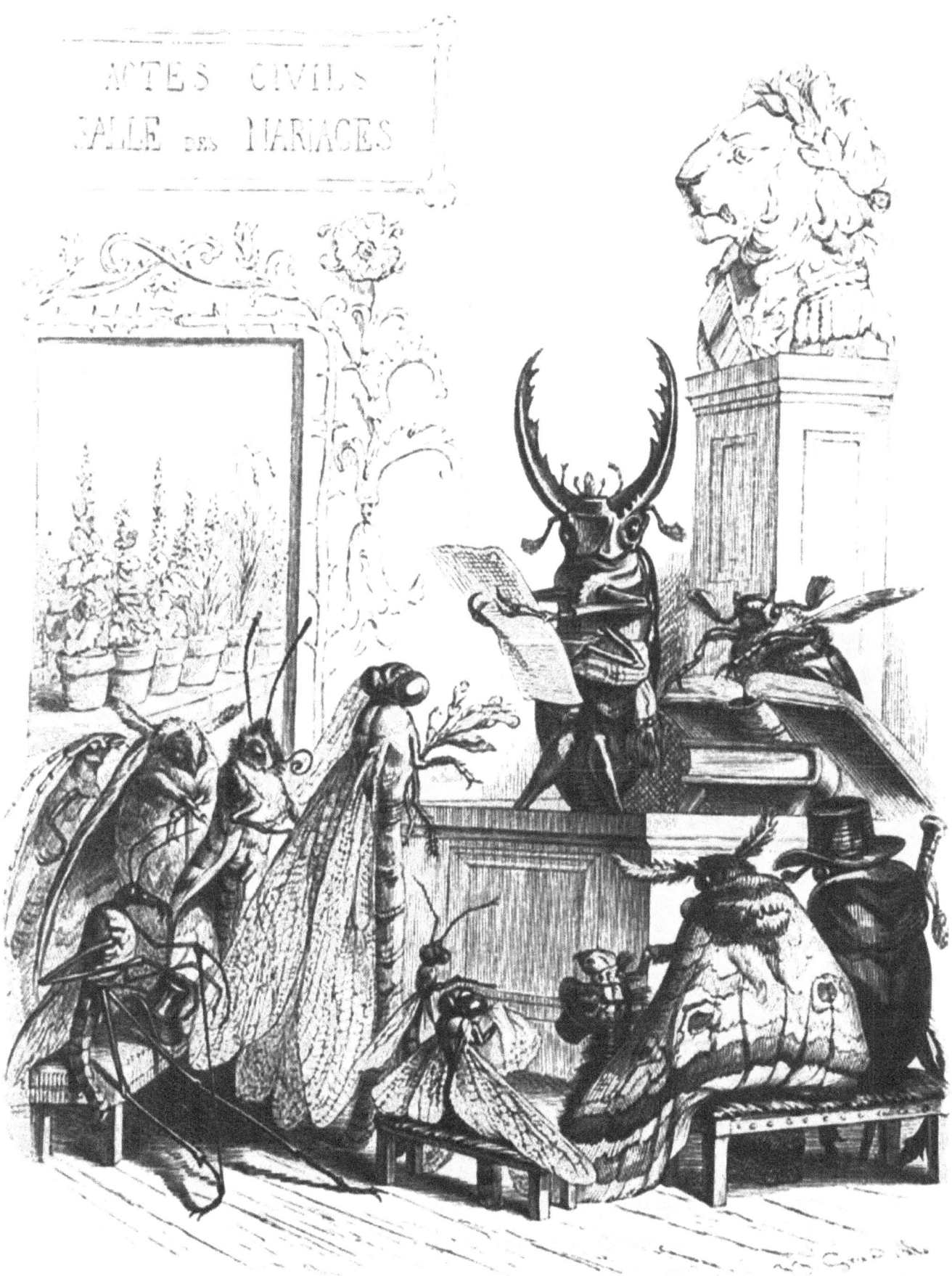

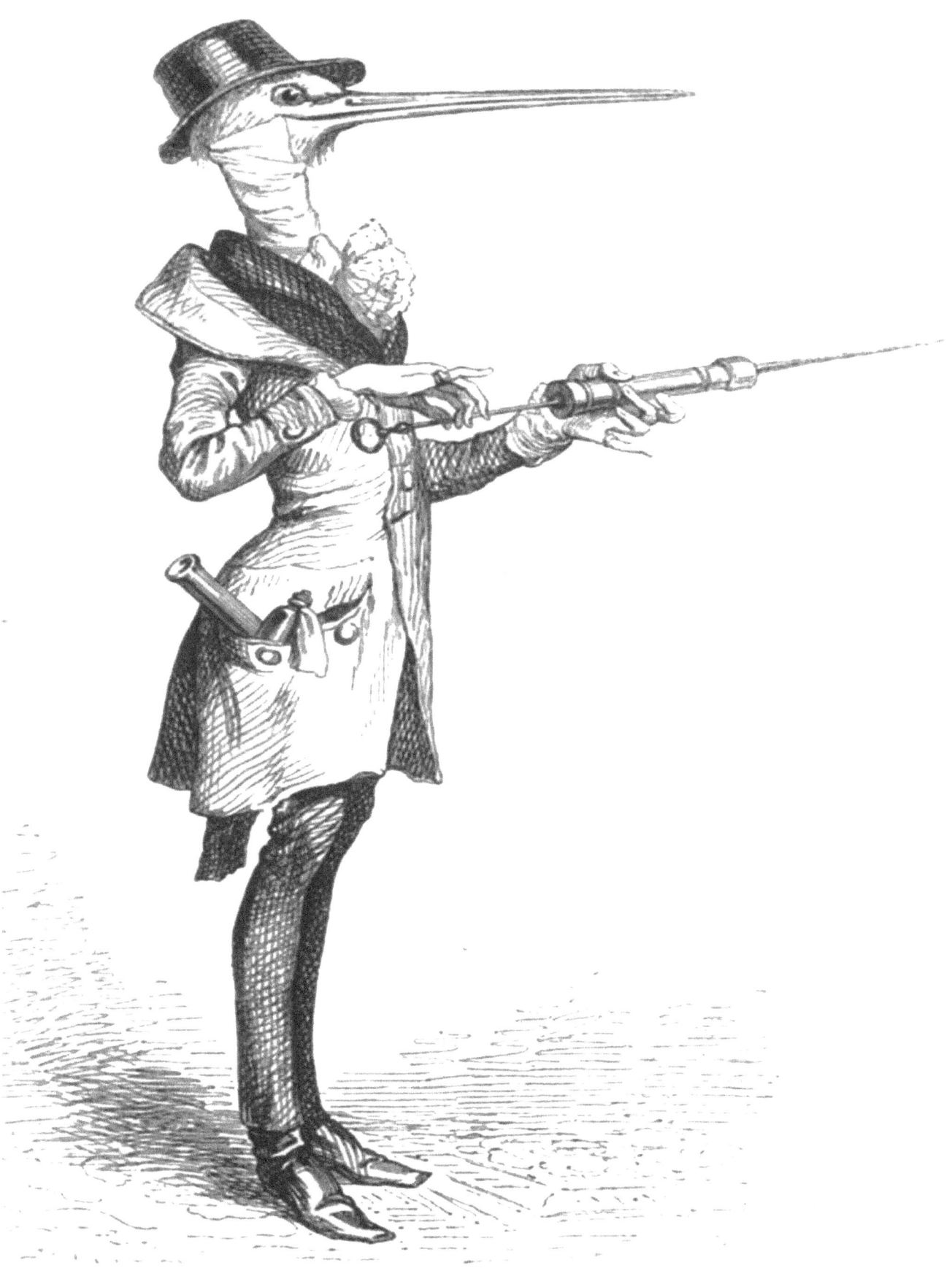

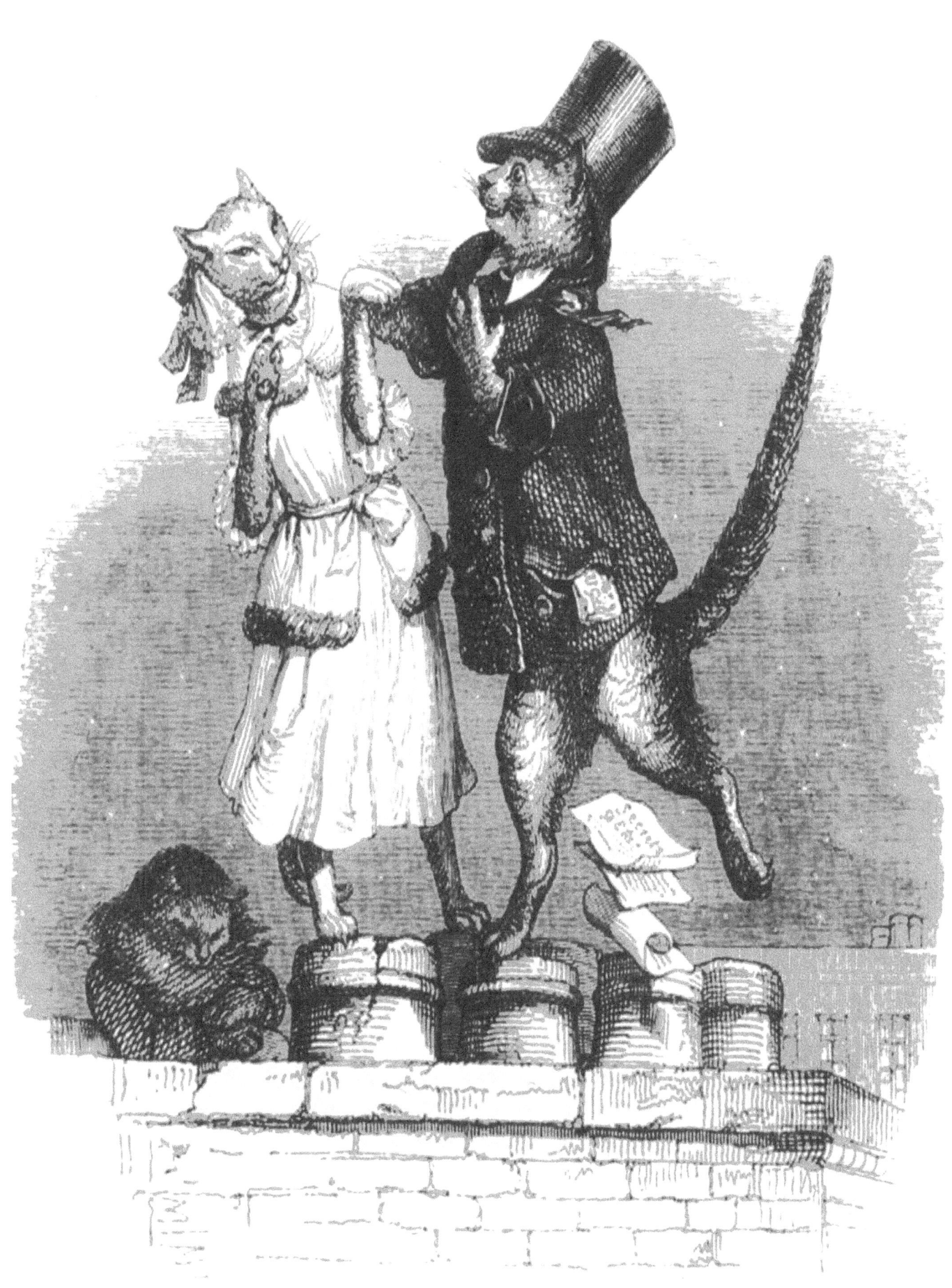

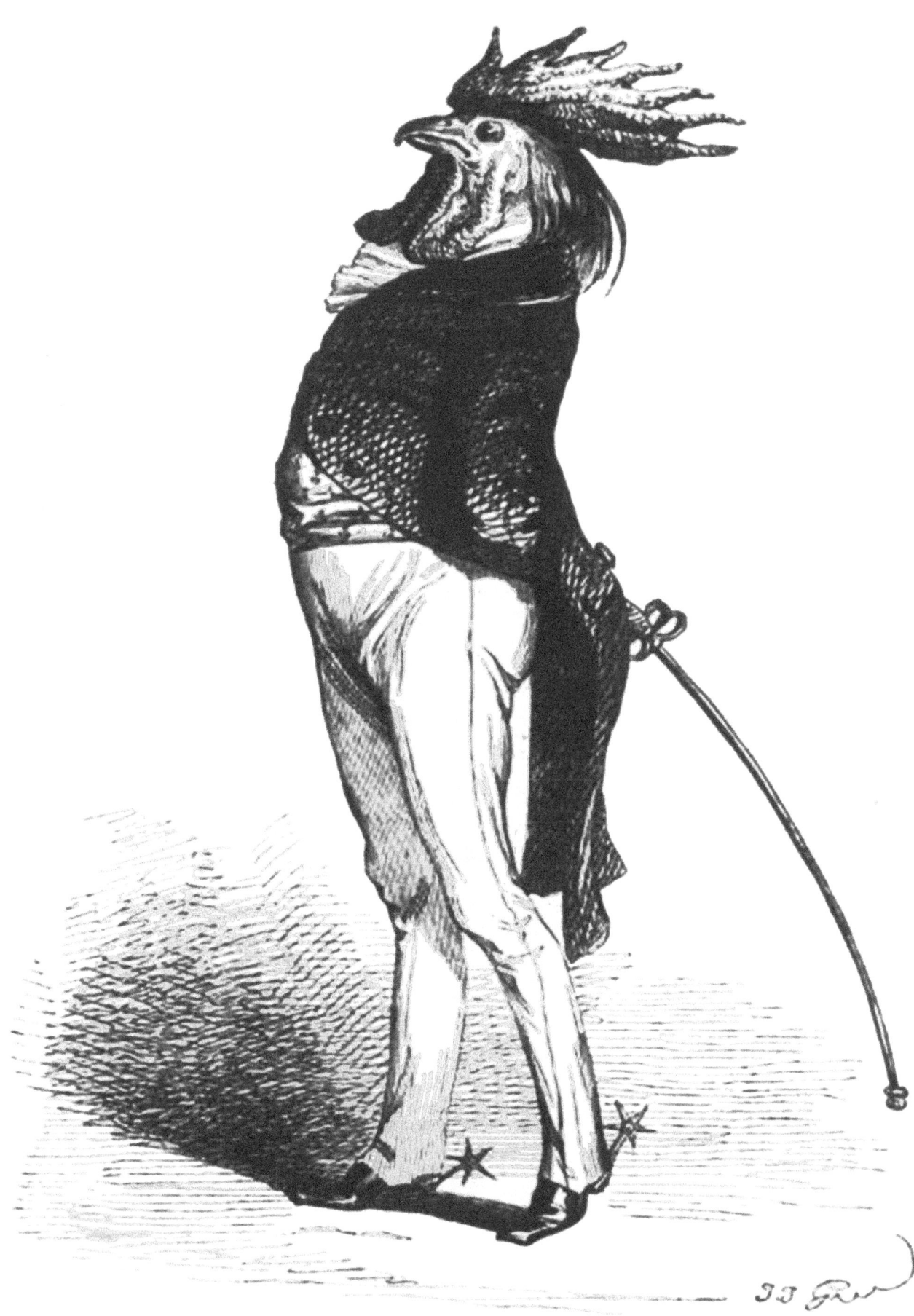

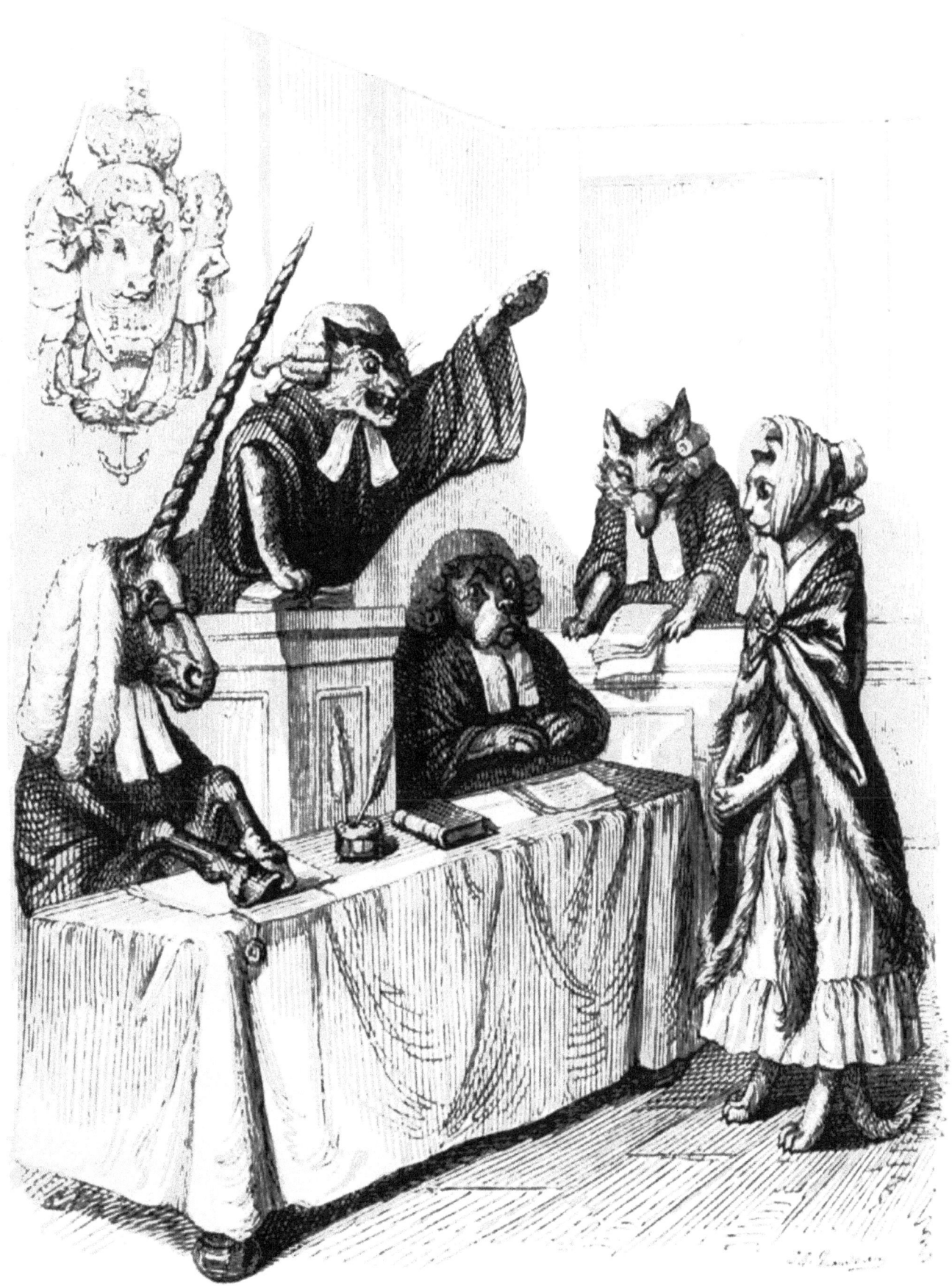

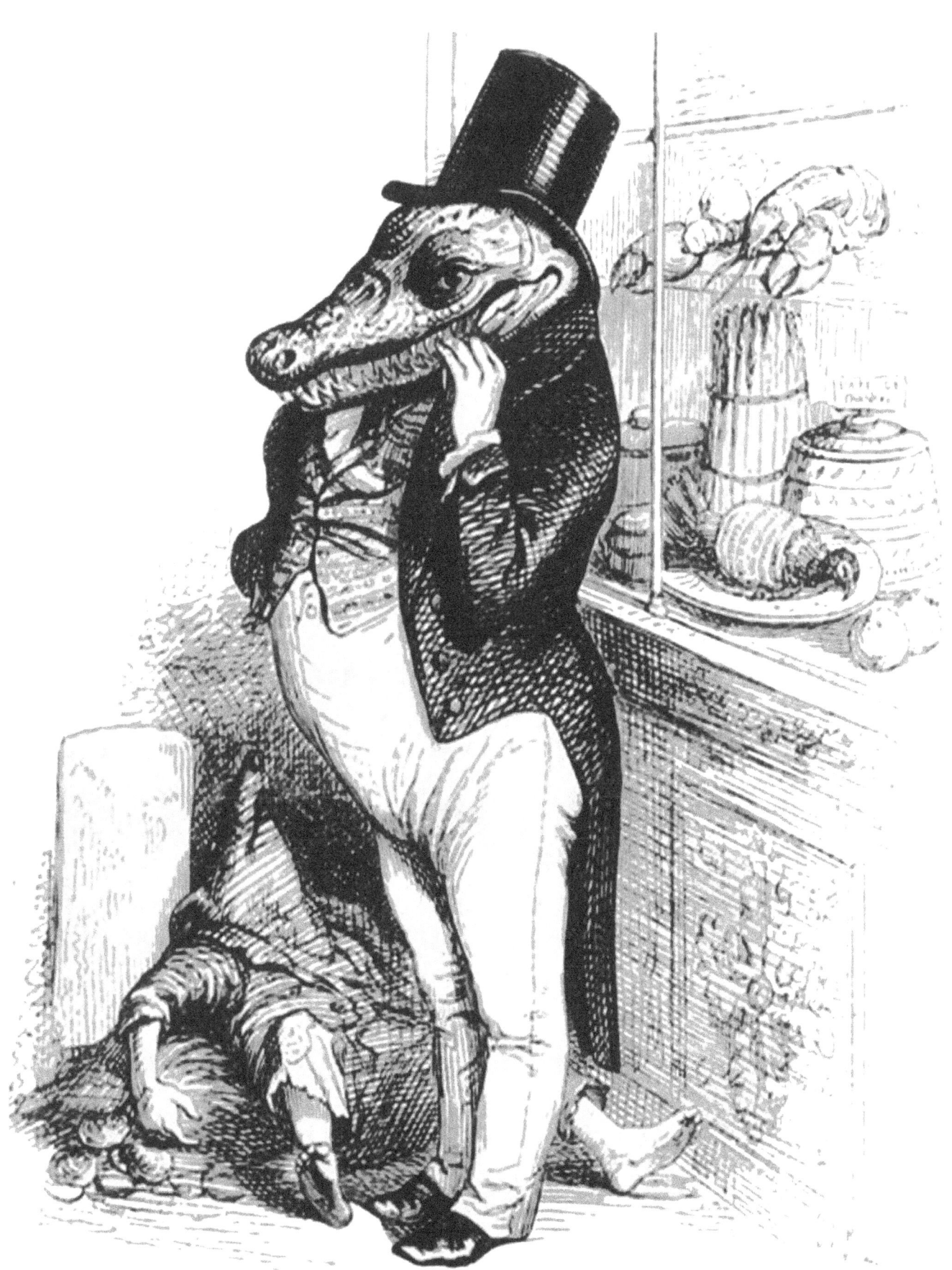

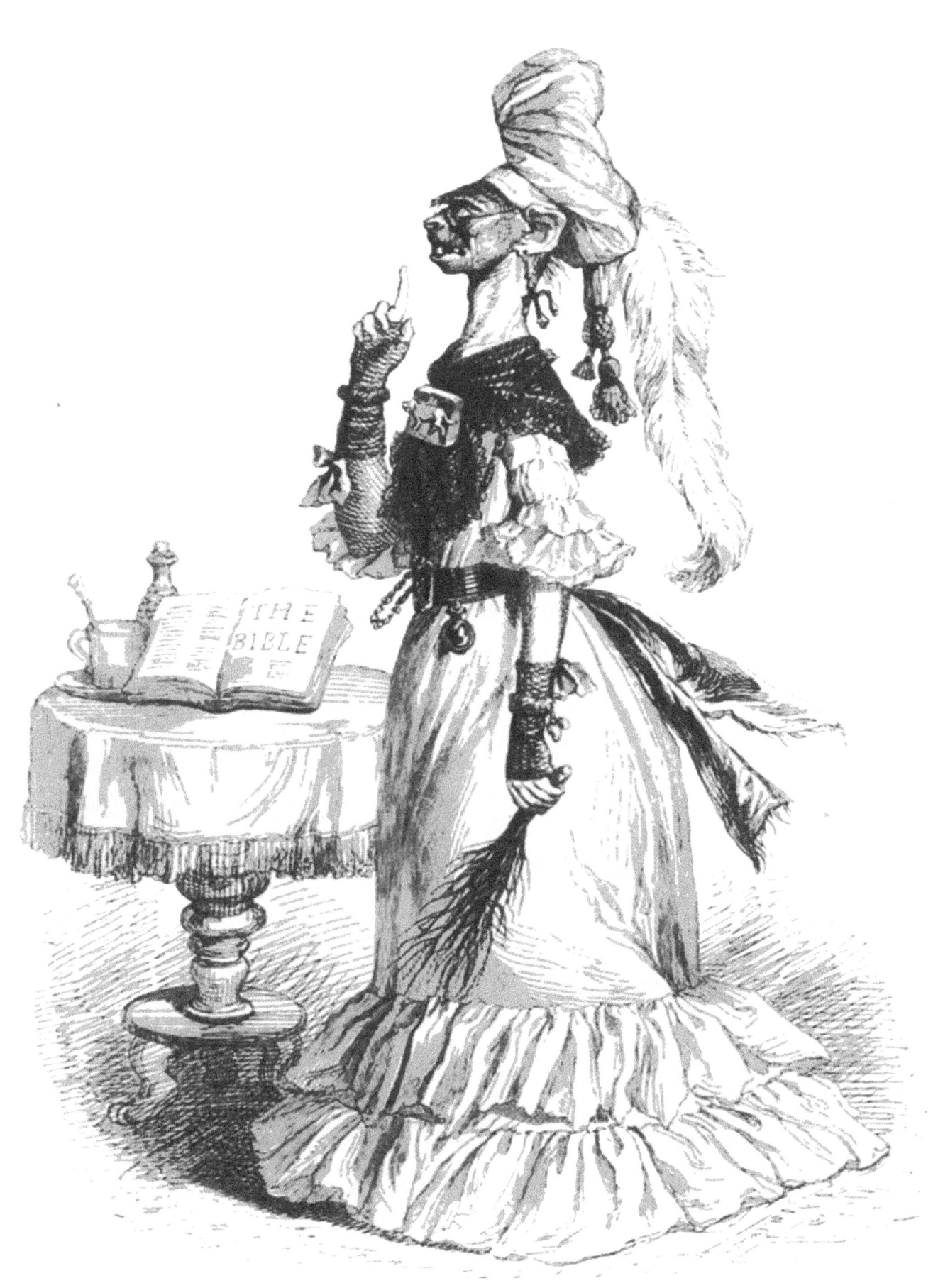

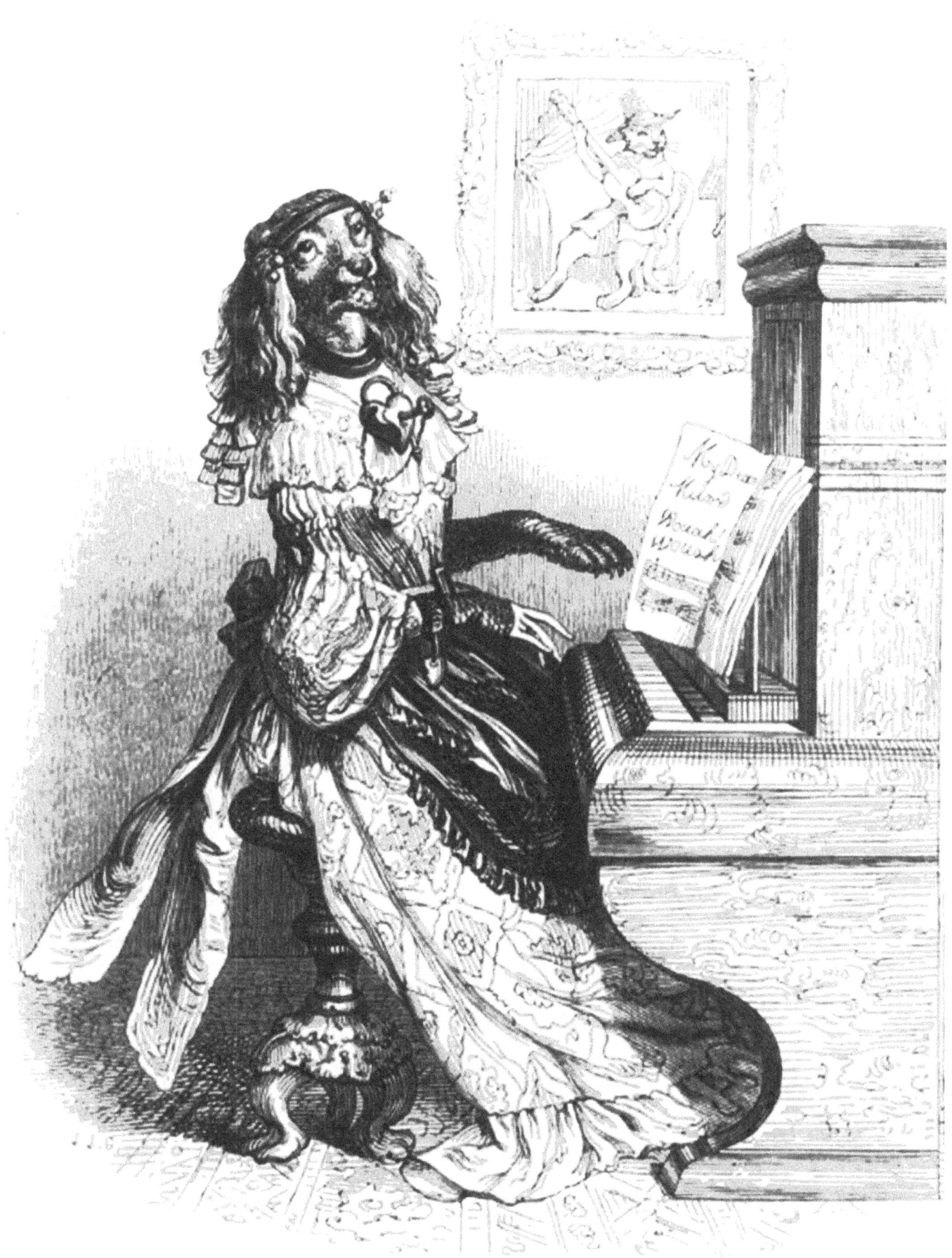

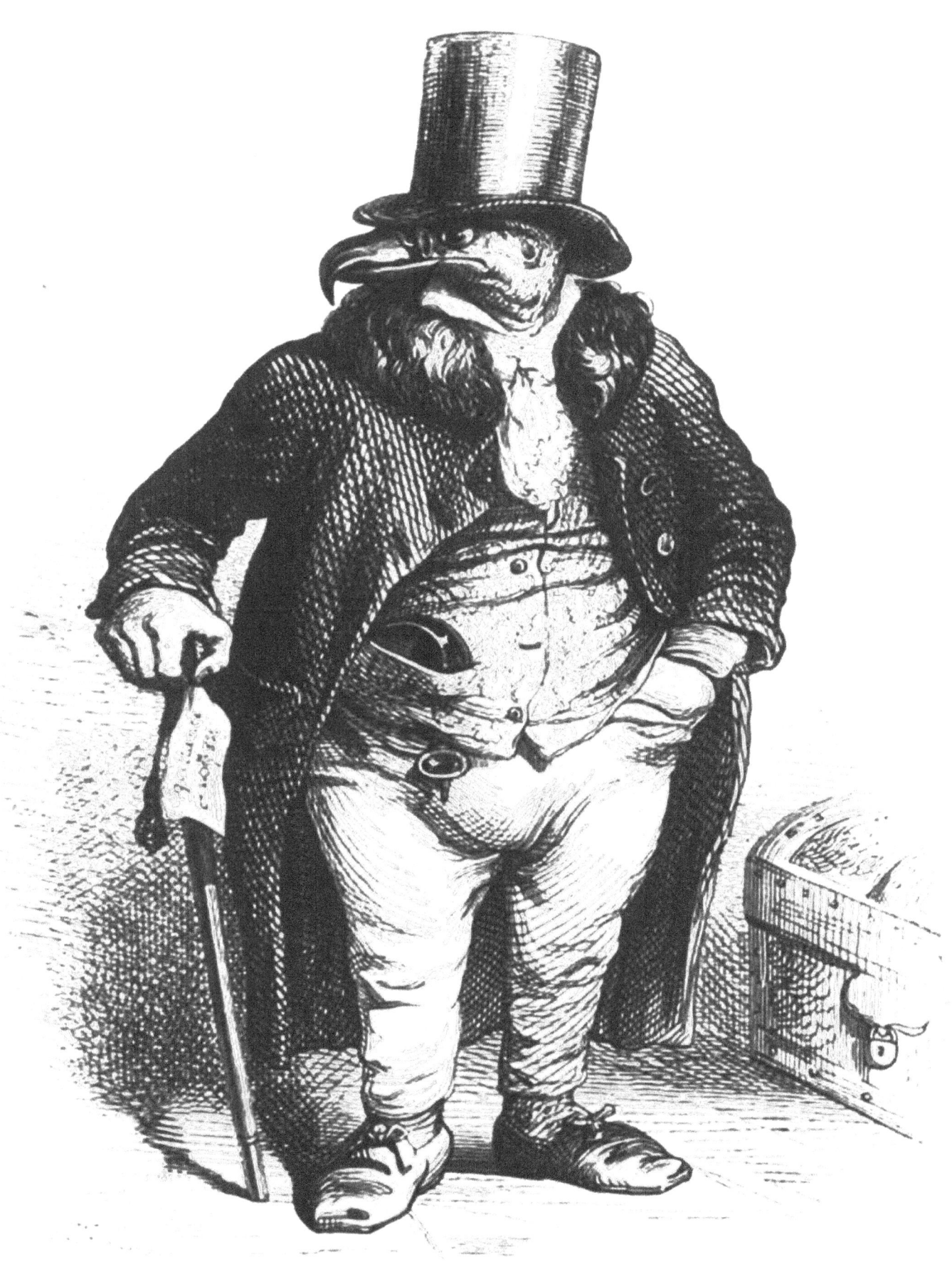

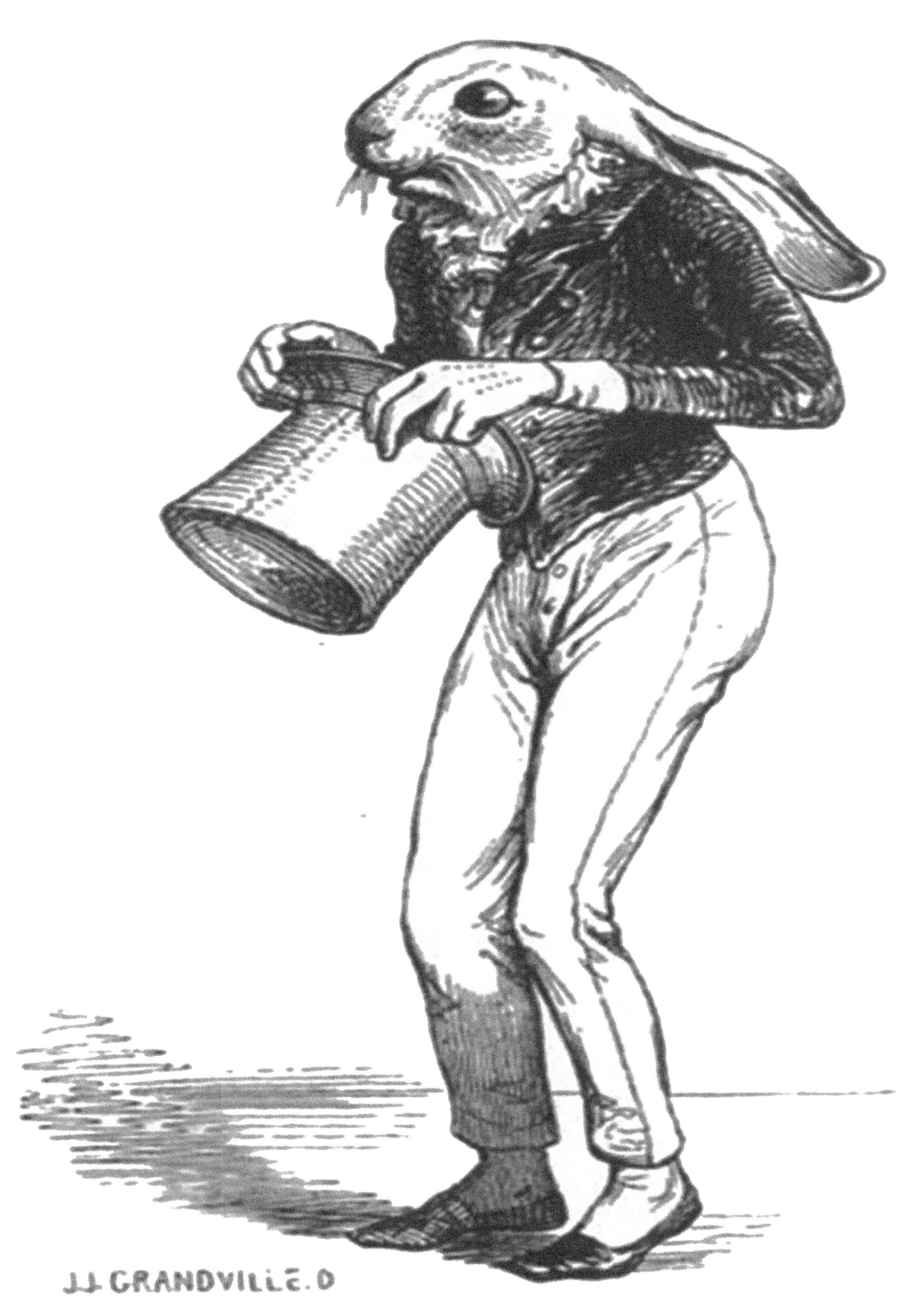

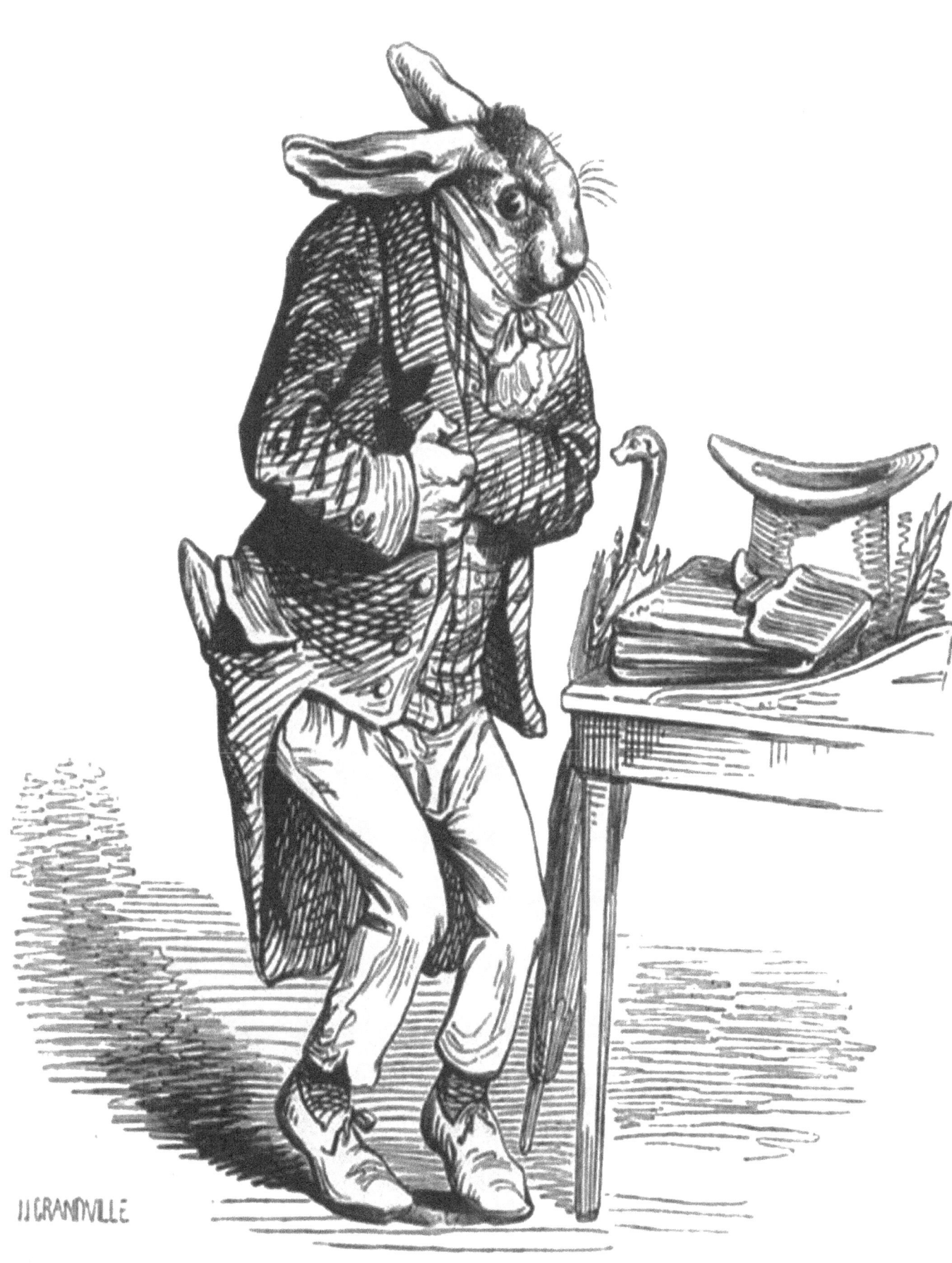

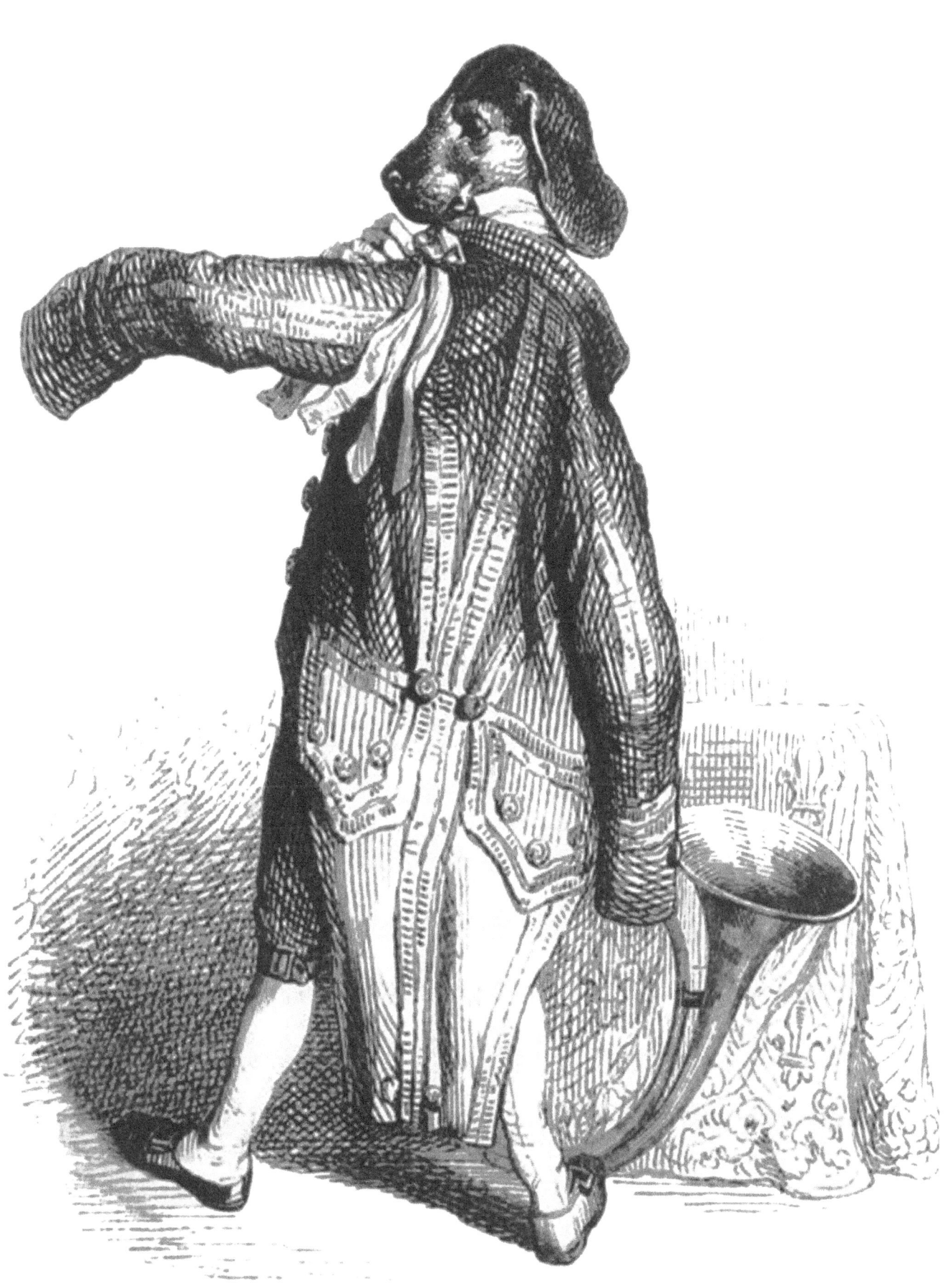

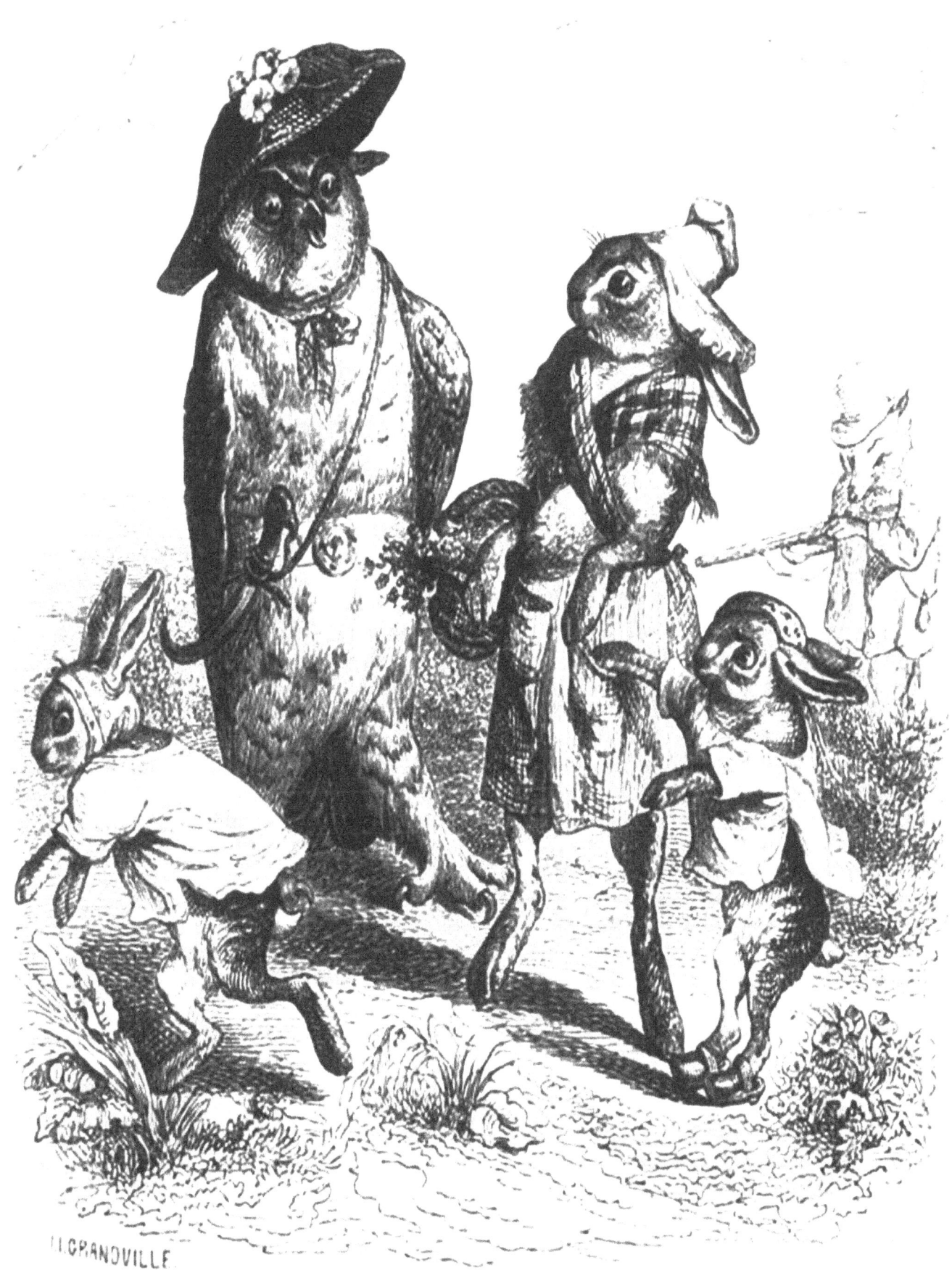

L.L.GRANDVILLE

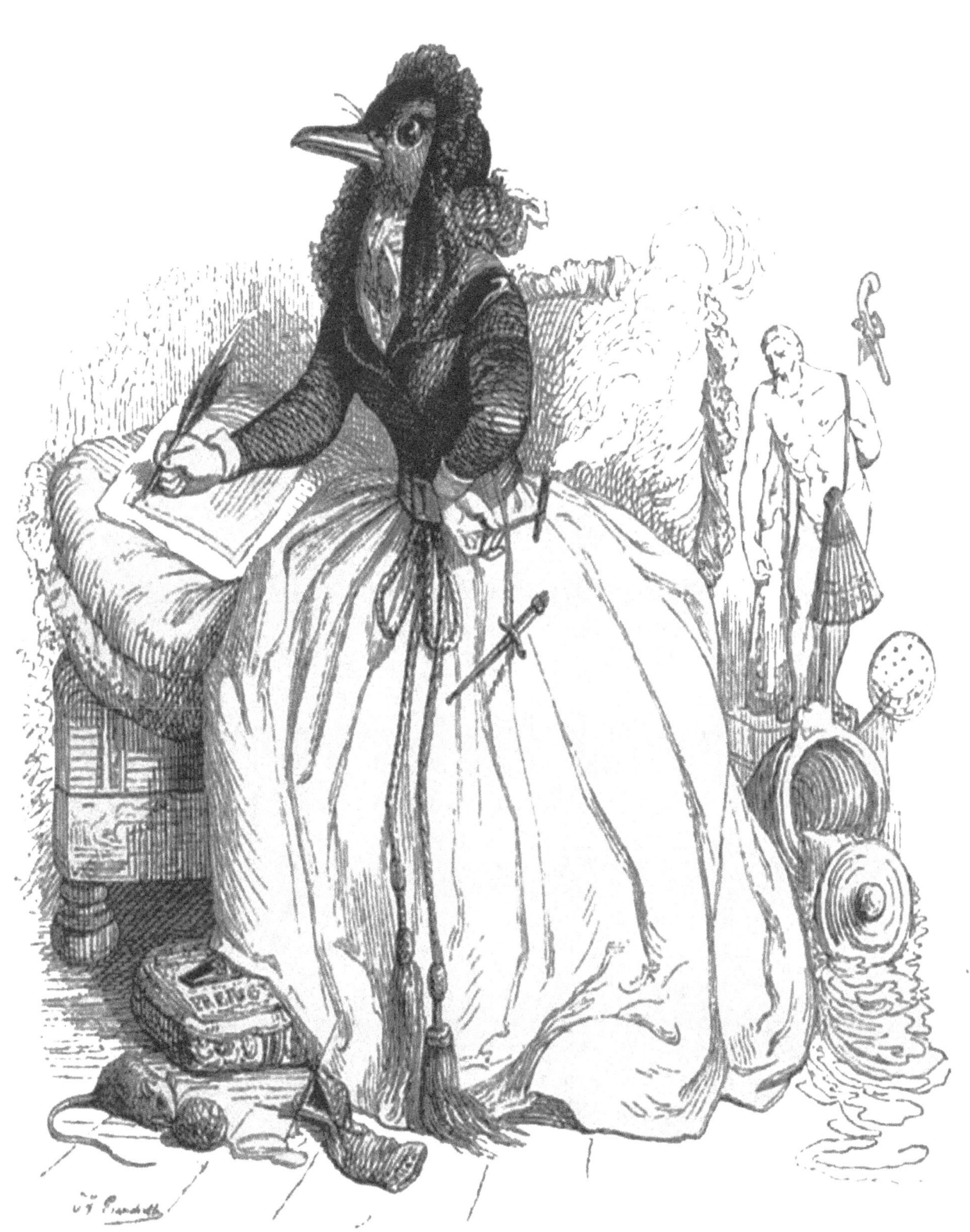

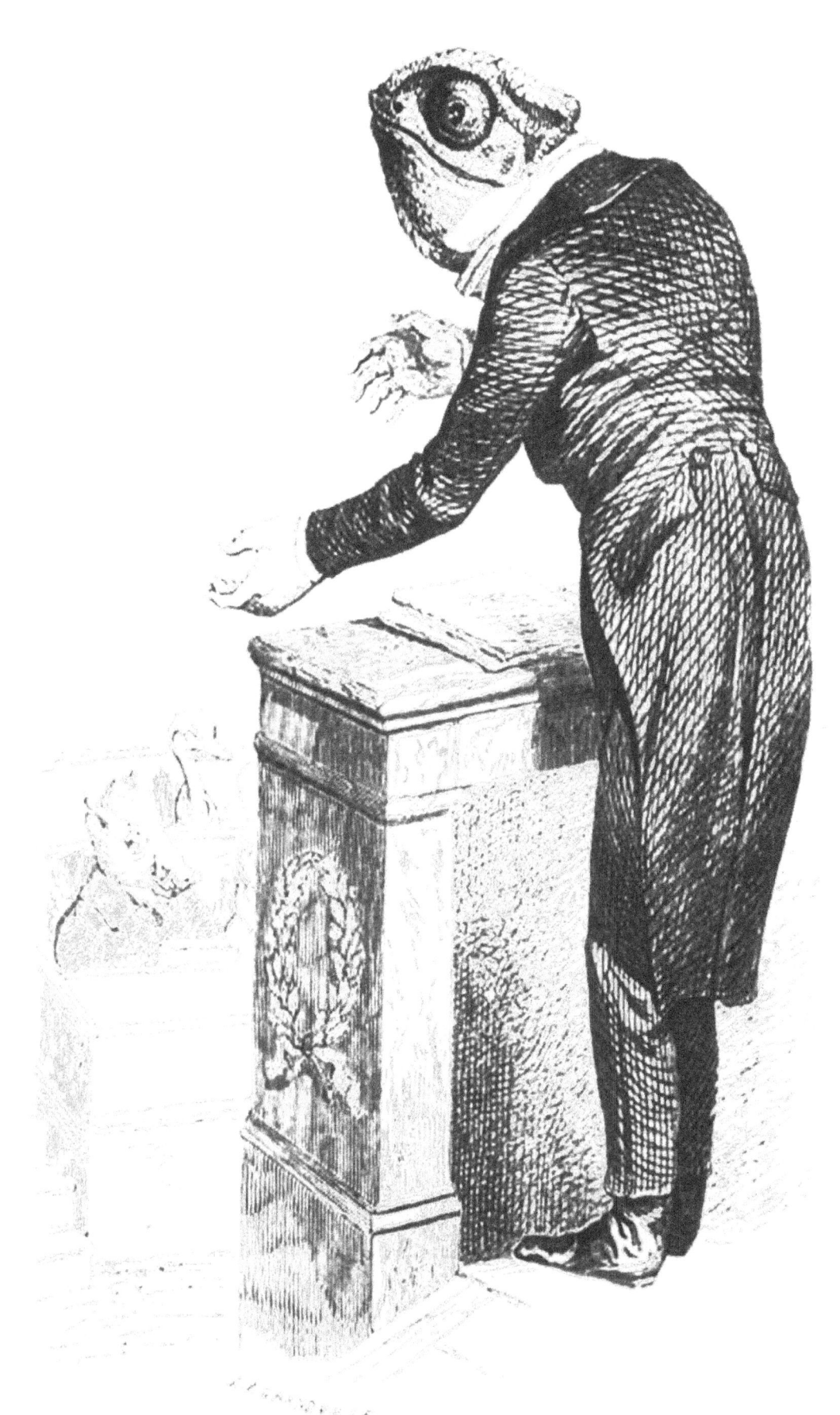

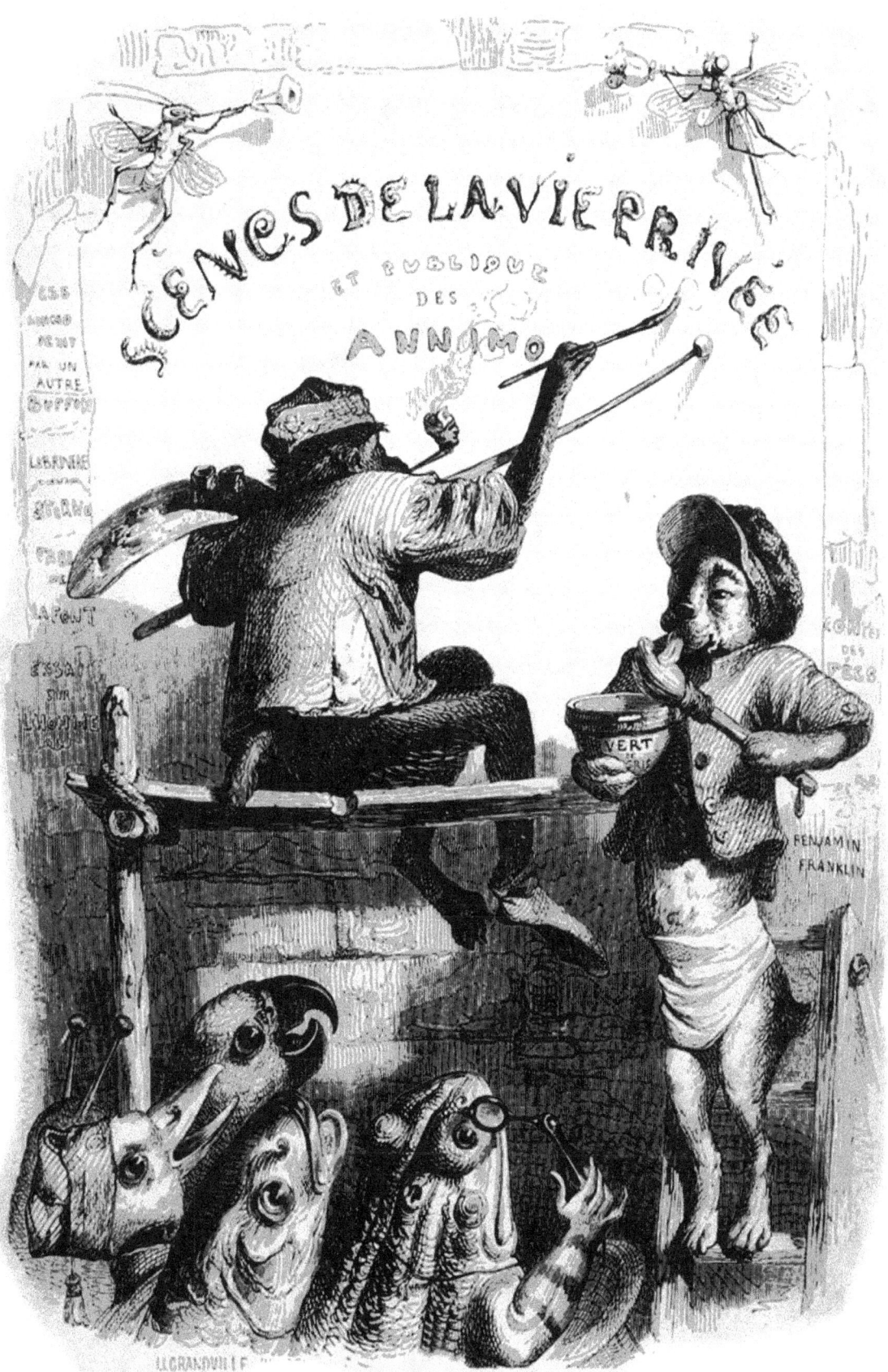